TECHNOLOGY BRINGS SOCIAL ADVANTAGES OR DISADVANTAGES

JOHN LOK

Made with ♥ on the Notion Press Platform
www.notionpress.com

Contents

Foreword

Introduction

In our societies , any kinds of products or services must need to apply demand and supply economic theory to analyze whether the kind of product or service may be value to invent to sell or serve to their customers in consumer market, if the kind of product or service demand number is less, then it ought not to raise manufacturing number to avoid "low price " sale or if the kind of product demand number is more, then it ought raise manufacturing number to have enough number in order to raise " high price" sale to satisfy customers their needs to buy their products.However, whether your product or serive's demand number depends on supply number or your product or service's supply number depends on demand number in order to make ths sale price is reasonable high or low level and reasonable supply number valuation.

Our business society had developed long time from farming period to manufacturing period, then to service industry period, till to nowadays technology service and manufacturing period. It brings this question: Can technology or human behavior may influence economic development? Human ourselves foolish or enjoyment behavior whether which can bring economic recession? If human can forgive to do enjoyment behavior, we can help economic growth? I shall apply behavioral economic theory to indicate cases to attempt to explain these questions.

Prologue

Contents

    Chapter 1 Explaining supply and demand economic theory relationship
The difference between past and nowadays economists their demand and supply economic theory explanation?
What are the relationship between demand and supply?
p.3-20
    Chapter 2 Human social job change demand and supply relationship
Why social behavior may influence organizational strategy needs to be changed p.21-51

Human Behavioral network job brings social
economic benefits
    What does human network job mean
    Why human network job behavior may influence economy

Robots take our jobs behavioral and economy influences
    Robot job behavior brings economy influences

Chapter 3 Human intellectual demand and supply behavior relationship
Intellectual human economic behaviors p.52-74
What does intellectual human economic behaviors
mean ?
    The relationship between social change and human
behavior

Chapter 4
Technology or human behavior whether may influence economic growth or recession

Human Behavioral network job brings social
economic benefits
    What does human network job mean
    Why human network job behavior may influence economy

Robots take our jobs behavioral and economy influences

Robot job behavior brings economy influences
p.75-90
Intellectual human economic behaviors
What does intellectual human economic behaviors
mean ?
The relationship between social change and human
behavior
How human productive behavior may influence economic development

● New Zealand farmer individual wine productive behavior
● America high technological productive behavior
● China share market investing behavior
Why has any individual country have many people invest share behavior which can influence the country's macro consumption desire?
Can technology influence human shopping behavioral change?
p.91-116
Why and how human behavior may influence the country's economic growth or recession?
Technology how impacts human behavior changing?
How and why employees behaviors may influence economy development?
Robots invention whether they can help organizations to raise efficiencies or inefficiencies?
Why social behavior may influence organizational strategy needs to be changed ?
How and why human behavior may influence economic growth or recession?
Reasons why human behavior may influence economic recession or growth ?
p.117-135
Chapter 5
Labors behavior or robot improves organizational performance

Reasons organizations need to raise employee individual performance
● Reasons why a company shouldn't ignore Performance Appraisals
● Considerations When Giving Employees Raises Performance, what benefits organizations
can earn
● Using Base Wages to Give Raises

● Performance-Linked Raises Performance.
● Merit-Based Raises and Your Compensation Package Can Raise Employee Individual Performance
● Reviewing Your Compensation Package
● Five Ways to Monitor Employee Performance Can Bring Your Organization Long Time Raising Efficiency And Productivity
● Learning Employee individual emotion feeling in performance evaluation
● How do organizations need to determine pay raises for employees as well as why it has relationship to improve performance ? p.136-155

How organizational structure influences
employee individual performance
● How organizational Structure can influence organizational behavior or employee individual performance?
● Reasons organization structure influence employee performance
● Why does Reward management (RM) need?
● APPRAISAL METHODS Management By Objective
● The Effects of Organizational Structure on Behavior p.156-170

Negative influences to lacking evaluating
performance organizatons
● Harm to employee emotion
● Impact of Compensation on Employee Performance
● Building employee Self-Confidence and Performance
● Can performance review raise employee confidence
● How to establish good or effective performance review to raise employee confidence to work ? p.171-186

Essentials of organizational behavioral learning
● Mc Donald soft skill organizational behavior
● Convenient framework of analysis of organizational behavior
● How to apply hard skill and soft skill to solve inefficient problem?
Essentials of robotic organizational behavioral learning
Artificial intelligence and customer service relationship
● How to apply robotic to raise customer service
performance p.187-200
● How robotic improves client communication

● How robotic and workers coordination in factory condition
● How and why robotic participation can bring personnel selection benefit
● Why can robotic bring talent working place benefit and reduces long time training and development cost
● How to implement the mind of strategy skills to robotic?
● How robotic can manufacturing and service
job market?
● How artificial intelligence influence e-business
workers market?
● How robotic becomes one kind of factor of production to the owning robotic task participation organizations?
● Why can robotic avoid productivity challenge and the firm does not need to employ extra worker ?
　How robotic brings positive and negative social change
● Why does robotic seem to McDonaldization franchise sale method
　● Why robotic seems to McDonaldization's operation?
　● Why does robotic seems to be common social commodity?
　● How can robotic bring global social stratification positive and negative change?
　Robotic how influences global economic change
● Encouraging new economic development
competitive factor
● How much robotic productivity can raise competition to cause effects of limited competition disadvantage to our society.
● How and why robotic brings long time intellectual development to global factories ?
● How can robotic help manufacturers to raise productivities or improve efficiency?
● Why does production possibilities curve may explain why robotic participation may assist few workers to raise productivities in factories ?

Must Developed And Developing Countries
Need Artificial Intelligent To Replace Human Job
● How AI help developing countries to communication and agriculture and learning and medical delivery development
　● Emergency Response to developing countries' earthquake natural damage sudden occurrence predicting
● Smart AI Agriculture

CHAPTER ONE

Explaining supply and demand economic theory relationship

The difference between past and nowadays economists their demand and supply economic theory explanation?

The law of supply and demand defines the relationship between the price of a given good or product and the willingness of people to either buy or sell it. Generally, as the price of a good increases, people are willing to supply more and demand less. These economists had explained economic demand and supply theory as below:

Philosopher John Locke is credited with one of the earliest written descriptions of this economic principle in his 1691 publication, Some Considerations of the Consequences of the Lowering of Interest and the Raising of the Value of Money. Locke addressed the concept of supply and demand as part of a discussion about interest rates in 17th-century England. Many merchants wanted the government to lower the cap on interest rates charged by private lenders so that people could borrow more money and thus purchase more goods. Locke argued that the free-market economy should set rates because government regulation could have unintended consequences. If the lending industry were left alone, interest rates would regulate themselves, Locke wrote: "The price of any commodity rises or falls by the proportion of the number of buyers and sellers."

Sir James Steuart's Inquiry into the Principles of Political Economy, published in 1796, was the first known printed use of the term "supply and demand." When Steuart wrote his treatise on political economy, one of his main concerns was the impact of supply and demand on laborers.

Adam Smith dealt extensively with the topic in his 1776 epic economic work, The Wealth of Nations. Often referred to as the Father of Economics, Smith explained the concept of supply and demand as an "invisible hand" that naturally guides the economy. According to Smith, the invisible hand is the automatic pricing and distribution mechanisms in the economy. Smith described a society in which bakers and butchers provide products that individuals need and want, providing a supply that meets demand and developing an economy that benefits everyone. It is important to note that Smith's ideas haven't gone without critique over the years since his ideas were first published, though. Over time, his ideas have been added to in order to represent the changing times and include concepts such as marginal utility, comparative advantage, entrepreneurship, the time-preference theory of interest, and monetary theory.

One of Marshall's most important contributions to microeconomics was his introduction of the concept of price elasticity of demand, which examines how price changes affect demand. In theory, people buy less of a particular product if the price increases, but Marshall noted that in real life, this behavior was not always true. The prices of some goods can increase without reducing demand, which means their prices are inelastic. Inelastic goods tend to include items such as medication or food that consumers deem crucial to daily life. Marshall argued that supply and demand, costs of production, and price elasticity all work together.

Nowadays economists they explain demand and supply economic theory, they have some different to past economists whose explanation as below:

How Does Supply and Demand Work? The law of supply and demand is a theory that explains the interaction between the sellers of a resource and the buyers of that resource. Generally, as price increases, people are willing to supply more and demand less and vice versa when the price falls. What does the bottom line mean. Despite the origins of the law of supply and demand beginning hundreds of years ago, it's still a topic frequently referenced and utilized today in economic theory and discussions. The theory has developed over time to accommodate recent technological and economical advancements, but the basic ideas of the theory remain largely the same.

Does demand depend on supply?

Supply and Demand Determine the Price of Goods and Quantities Produced and Consumed. Consumers may exhaust the available supply of a good by purchasing a given good or service at a high volume. This leads to an increase in demand. As demand increases, the available supply also decreases.

What does market demand depend on?

Market factors affecting demand of consumer goods. The demand for a good increases or decreases depending on several factors. This includes the product's price, perceived quality, advertising spend, consumer income, consumer confidence, and changes in taste and fashion.

Who controls the demand in supply and demand?

Supply and demand are in turn determined by technology and the conditions under which people operate. At one extreme, the market could be populated by a large number of virtually identical sellers and buyers (for example, the market for ballpoint pens).

What are the two laws of demand and supply?

The law of demand holds that the demand level for a product or a resource will decline as its price rises, and rise as the price drops. Conversely, the law of supply says higher prices boost supply of an economic good while lower ones tend to diminish it.

What factors affect demand and supply?

Price fluctuations are a strong factor affecting supply and demand. When a product gets expensive enough that the average consumer no longer feels it is worth it to buy the product, then the demand declines. This leads to cuts in production that will hopefully stabilize the product's value.

What factors affect demand and demand?

Demand may be defined as the quantity of a commodity that a consumer is able and willing to buy, at each possible price, over a given period of time. • Essential elements of demand are quantity, ability, willingness, prices, and period of time.

Which factors affect supply?

Generally, the supply of a product depends on its price and other variables such as the cost of production.

    a. Price. Price can be understood as what the consumer is willing to pay to receive a good or service. ...

b. Cost of production. ...

c. Technology. ...

d. Governments' policies. ...

e. Transportation condition.

How does supply and demand work together?

It's a fundamental economic principle that when supply exceeds demand for a good or service, prices fall. When demand exceeds supply, prices tend to rise. There is an inverse relationship between the supply and prices of goods and services when demand is unchanged.

What happens to supply when demand increases?

An increase in demand, all other things unchanged, will cause the equilibrium price to rise; quantity supplied will increase. A decrease in demand will cause the equilibrium price to fall; quantity supplied will decrease.

What is the theory of demand?

Demand theory describes the way that changes in the quantity of a good or service demanded by consumers affects its price in the market, The theory states that the higher the price of a product is, all else equal, the less of it will be demanded, inferring a downward sloping demand curve.

What are the 4 basic laws of supply and demand?

1) If the supply increases and demand stays the same, the price will go down. 2) If the supply decreases and demand stays the same, the price will go up. 3) If the supply stays the same and demand increases, the price will go up. 4) If the supply stays the same and demand decreases, the price will go down.

The different types of demand are as follows:

i. Individual and Market Demand: ...

ii. Organization and Industry Demand: ...

iii. Autonomous and Derived Demand: ...

iv. Demand for Perishable and Durable Goods: ...

v. Short-term and Long-term Demand:

What creates demand for a product?

You can create demand for a unique product if you can manage to solve a persistent problem for the consumer. People are always running away from pain, and providing them with an outlet is a sure-fire way to create massive demand for your goods.

What are the 7 factors that affect supply?

The seven factors which affect the changes of supply are as follows: (i) Natural Conditions (ii) Technical Progress (iii) Change in Factor Prices (iv) Transport Improvements (v) Calamities (vi) Monopolies (vii) Fiscal Policy.

What can affect demand?

Factors Affecting Demand

Price of the Product. ...

The Consumer's Income. ...

The Price of Related Goods. ...
The Tastes and Preferences of Consumers. ...
The Consumer's Expectations. ...
The Number of Consumers in the Market.
What are the three factors affecting demand?
The demand for a product will be influenced by several factors:
Price. Usually viewed as the most important factor that affects demand.
...
Income levels. ...
Consumer tastes and preferences. ...
Competition. ...
Fashions.
What are the 4 factors of supply?
The four factors that can shift the supply curve include natural conditions, input prices, technology, and government.
What causes increase in supply?
If the cost of production is lower, the profits available at a given price will increase, and producers will produce more. With more produced at every price, the supply curve will shift to the right, meaning an increase in supply.
What causes supply changes?
A change in supply is an economic term that describes when the suppliers of a given good or service alter production or output. A change in supply can occur as a result of new technologies, such as more efficient or less expensive production processes, or a change in the number of competitors in the market.
Is supply and demand a good strategy?
When it comes to profit placement, supply and demand zones can be a great tool as well. Always place your profit target ahead of a zone so that you don't risk giving back all your profits when the open interest in that zone is filled.
How is demand created?
Demand creation is a process that fuels the revenue pipeline so the sales team can meet or exceed their quotas. In other words, it takes your big idea — the creative appeal of your brand — and turns it into sales. That sounds a lot like demand generation, which often gets confused with lead generation.
What are the two parts of demand?
Economists define demand as the quantity of a good or service that buyers are willing and able to buy at all possible prices during a certain time period.

Notice that there are two components to demand: willingness to purchase and ability to pay.

Can we control demand?

If you're willing to think and act strategically, you can easily manipulate the laws of supply and demand. It should be surprising to learn, however, that by manipulating the laws of supply and demand, you can make more profit in less time and with far fewer headaches

How do you control demand?

Here are five short-term actions to improve your demand variability management plans in this time of uncertainty:

Maintain transparent, proactive relationships with your suppliers. ...

Activate alternate sources of supply. ...

Reduce lead times. ...

Update inventory policy and planning. ...

Align supply and demand management.

What are the 8 types of demand?

There are 8 states of demand: negative demand, no demand, latent demand, falling demand, irregular demand, full demand, overfull demand and unwholesome demand.

What is Demand?

Types of Determinants of Demand. Every factor has a unique impact on demand. ...

Price of the Product. ...

The Income of the Consumers. ...

Number of Buyers in the Market. ...

Consumer's Expectations. ...

Tastes and Preferences of The Consumers. ...

Complement Goods. ...

Substitute Product.

What is theory of supply?

The law of supply is a fundamental principle of economic theory which states that, keeping other factors constant, an increase in price results in an increase in quantity supplied. In other words, there is a direct relationship between price and quantity: quantities respond in the same direction as price changes.

What are the types of supply?

There are five types of supply—market supply, short-term supply, long-term supply, joint supply, and composite supply.

Which comes first supply or demand?

Demand comes first and it's followed by the corresponding supplies. Supply and demand are both very important to economic activity. Supply is the total amount of a particular good or service available at a given time to consumers at a given price. Demand is a representation of a consumer's desire to purchase goods and services; it acts as a measurement of a consumer's willingness to purchase a specific good or service at a given price. These two economic forces influence each other; they are both important for the economy because they impact the prices of consumer goods and services within an economy and the quantities produced and consumed. Supply and demand are both keys to understanding the economy because they reflect the prices and quantities of consumer goods and services within an economy.

What are the relationship between demand and supply?

According to market economy theory, the relationship between supply and demand balances out at a point in the future; this point is called the equilibrium price.

Economists and companies analyze the relationship between supply and demand when making strategic product decisions. Both economists and companies analyze the relationship between supply and demand when making strategic product decisions. The assumption behind a market economy is that supply and demand are the best determinants for an economy's growth and health.

Consumer Behavior Influences Demand

One way that companies or economists might analyze this relationship is to create graphs that chart the equilibrium price of certain goods and services in order to determine product development and their production schedule. Consumer behavior dictates which products are produced and sold because consumers create the demand that companies attempt to meet. As a result, companies may study consumer behavior in an attempt to understand the current demand and predict future demand. It is vital that companies maintain the capacity to produce enough of a good or service that they can satisfy consumer demands.

Supply and demand are two sides of the same market coin. Generally, supply is how much of something is available or will be produced at a certain price. Demand is how much of something people want to purchase or consume at a certain price. One way to develop a more precise relationship between the two is to consider how the price of something affects its supply and its demand. Generally when the price of a good goes up, so does the supply, since firms are willing to create more when they can sell at higher prices. But when the price of a good goes up consumers will, at the same time, generally demand less. It is the interaction of supply and demand that determines how much will be produced and consumed and at what price, converging to a state known as equilibrium.

CHAPTER TWO

Human social job change demand and supply relationship

The relationship between social change and human behavior

Human Behavioral network job brings social economic benefits

Whether human social job change it depends on social job demand more or job supply more? What does human network job mean ? Why may human network job be popular? Why human network job behavior may influence economy ?

Nowadays internet is popular to use. We can apply internet to find data , search any new things, even earn money. Why does internet may become huma network job source. For example, e-publish may be one kind of new human network job. Any authors may apply internet channel to help them to sell electronic or paper books from e-publisher web store. They may apply facebook, you tub etc. any online channel to promote themselves new books to let new readers to know whether when they may buy themselves favourable new topic books to read from electronic publisher web store.

Thus, future electronic publisher industry may help any authors to build internet network platform to help them to sell and promote ot advertise their any one new electronic or paper book topic to let global any one reader to choose to buy their any new topic books from electronic publisher web store easily and conveniently. However, it implies that electronic network platform author may be one kind of future new human network job in our societies.

How electronic network platform author job may bring economy benefit in macro economy view? A person can have few friends, contacts and still be very influential if these few

friends and contacts are themselves highly influential, e.g. one author must not need to know any one reader in global society. When they like to choose any electronic books from electronic internet network platform. They may become the author's any one topic book buyer, when they feel the author's any one topic book is fun and attract they make decision to buth the strange author whose the topic book from electronic book publisher's platform web store conventiently in short time. Although, they are strangers, they do not know themselves , but the reader can understand what it way that made Google from writing platofrm to create new creative mind and typing network job method to replace traditional hand writing book method for global authors. It will be one kind of new human network writing job.

Hence, global any one reader can apply an innovative search engine , such as google.com to find whether whom author personal new topic books are value to read from internet.

Then, the electroniuc publisher's web store may be new book store platform sale network to help the author to sell many electronic or paper books from electronic network platform

in short time. So, internet may be future new network plaform to help global any one author to create network writing job absolutely. Furthermore, internet may be popular social media

to help any one author to build goold relationship between his/her readers. It is one kind of new network, human network job. New authors do not need to buy many paper books to prepare to put in any one book shop warehouse. Their every book can print on demand to reduce out of book stock in any one book shop. They may choose to sell either electronic books or paper books both from any one book publisher web store. So, electronic network platform may be one kind of good writing channel to help human authors to create income and it can also help authors to bring new creative mind and new topic fun content books to let readers to know and buy to read from electronic publisher network platform.

Why does human behavior may be one kind of new human network job to bring global economic advantages. ALthough, it may be free income or without inocme, but the person does the network behavior, his/her behavior may be bring advantages to influence many other people's health. For this case, when a worker in a coffee shop in an airport gets a vaccination against the flu, it does not only helps him or her stay healthy, but also helps the many travellers who might otherwise have been inflected if that workers caught the flu. So, the externality , the result implies the vaccination of even a part of a community conveys benefits to the whole community. For example, governments pay special attention to the vaccinations of school children, teachers, health mothers, and the elderly, categories of people particularly susceptible not only to catching, but also to transmitting a disease.

It is not accidental that governments are heavily involved with vaccination . When there are externalities, free market, fail to persuade individual incentives with society's

their the worker's decision of whether to get a vaccine ends up attracting whether other people get sick. The workers might not fully take all these other people's potential suffering into account when making her or his vaccination decision.

As Stanford University does many suggestions, understand this and tries to help them make the right decisions and so providers free flu vaccines for its staff and students.

Small pockets of unvaccinated individuals can allow a disease to gain a spread more widely well-being. For example, parent weighing the costs and benefits of a vaccine for their child is not always thinking of the consequences of that vaccination to other people. THese are markets in which subsidizing or regulating behavior can make everyone better off. Because the reason for requiring that a child be vaccinated before enrolling in school is not just to protect that child, because each child's vaccination affects others via potential contagions.

On conclusion, it seems that many traditional paper book publish business begain to change to electronic book publish business. Due, to online technology existence, it influences many readers choose to buy electronic books to read. Hence, due to readers reading demand change which is from paper book reading habit to electonic book reading habit.Then,it explains that electornic book supply number depends on electronic book reader reading demand in economic view.

Robots take our jobs behavioral and economy influences

Robot job behavior brings economy influences

Whether robot labor needs are depended on employer labor demand more or robot labor number supply more? If one day robots can replace human to do simple, even complex jobs. They will bring what influences to our global societial economy.The popular economic refrain declares that the
global middle class is dying and robots will soon take our jobs, e.g. shopping center customer service jobs, library service jobs, cinema ticket sale jobs, restaurant kitchen cooker jobs,
even, bus drivers, taxi drivers etc. public transport driving jobs, accountant, doctors etc. professional jobs. Whether it is beautiful or petty matter if our future societies have many human jobs can be replaced to do from robots. Businessman must may reduce to employ employees and reduce to pay salary or wage, when robots can be replaced to do their employees tasks. But, societies must bring unemployement rate rises , due to societies will have many people loss jobs when their employers choose to buy robots to serve their clients or do any office tasks or customer service or cleaning etc. tasks.

In micro economy view, employers may save money in long term, but in macro economy view, it will cause unemployment ratio rises , even crime rate rises when there are many people lose
jobs in societies. These models of doom, though, fail to account for the hundreds of businesses riding the waves of change in their industries when robots may be invented to replace human to do many simple , even complex tasks in our future societies.

WE may image that one small factory needs to manufacture fishes canes to sell to supermarket, the small , cheaper stuff and higher margin parts of the fishes manufacture industry. Before, this factory needs to employe many human factory workers need to help every fresh customer makeing the perfect fishing gear, designed for performance, durability, and cost in order to achieve to manufacture every fish cane in whole fished processing manufacturing stages. Every worker needs to spend about 15 to twenty minutes to finish every fish cane , till to delivery to any supermarket to sell. If this fish canes manufacturing factory can apply manufacturing robots to help them to finish any one working tasks , every robot can only spend five minutes to finish whole fresh fish cane manufacturing process. Thus, every robot can
help this factory save 10 to 15 minutes time to finsh every fish cane

manufacturing process. IN fact, time is money, because when every robot can help this factory to reduce 10 to 15 minutes time to compare human worker. Then, this factory can finish about 20 fish canes in one hour if it can use robot to help it to manufacture fish canes. Otherwise, if this factory still use human workers to help it to manufacture fish canes, then it can finsh about 3 to 4 fish canes in one hour. SO, the manufacturing efficiency ensures that robots must help this fish manufacturing factory to raise fish canes number more than human workers. So, in robotic behavioral economy view, manufacturing robots must help this fish canes manufacturing factory to raise fish canes manufacturing number and deliver increasing number to supermarkets to prepare to sell every day. Robots can help this fish canes manufacturing factory bring manufacturing time saving, rising manufacturing efficiency, improving performance and reducing wages expenditure long time advantages in micro economy view. However, manufacturing robots can also bring disadvanages to society, e.g. increasing unemployment ratio, increasing crime rate,
this factory workers will lose jobs and income, they need earn social welfare from government and increasing government finance pressure in short time, even long time in macro economic view.

Stanford University graduate program in economics, Scott lecturer explained that "in demand and supply economic theory for robots supply and demand case, robots supply number increasing may influence human workers demand number decrease. It sometimes calls " the efficient frontier".
No specific human beings were mentioned in any of economics classes. As robots supply and demand in market case, They (robots) may be purely theoretical " agents" who reached to the most reasonable sale prices in order to persuade any one businessman buyer to make manufacturing robot buying decision whether robots can help him / her to bring how much saving time , saving money, saving cost, improving performance, efficiency economic benefit before he/she plans to reduce workers number when he/she decides to apply robots to replace human workers in his/her factory or office or any service department, e.g. cinema ticket sale service, shopping center customer service, shopping center cleaning , supermarket customer service etc. service or sale tasks. When robots can replace human to do any one of these tasks in any organizations. So, robots may be human worker agents who reached to prices the way robots would react to a software command. There was nothing that explained why some people thrived

and others did n't or why truly brilliant, hardworking people could fail when much lazier folks succeeded." Having been admitted to the Stanford University graduate program in economics, Scott lecturer hoped to get his answers there.

How robots influence our future social changing? Using the right technology can be a boon to your business in this economy. For internet example, it is easier than ever to find well-matched customers all around the world, to stay in contact with them, and to more quickly design the products they want. If you focus solely on being cutting -edge, though you risk letting the technology

take over what should be very robust relationships with your customers , employees, and colleagues. IN nowaddays society, technoligical advances and cutomation, personal

relationships in business are more crucial than ever. I mean that robots can not replace human to serve clients to let them to feel more comfortable and passion more easily. For shoe shop case example, if the shoe shop apply one robot to serve its clients to replace human shoe salesperson to serve its shoe customers. Robots ensure that they can not persuade every shoe potential buyer to make shoe buying decision more easily when robots need to contact every shoe potential buyer. The reason is simple, because robots can not touch any one shoe buyer individual emotion very easier.

If the shoe buyer needs the robots to help him/her to choose any right shoe styles when he/she can not feel himself / herself can make the most right shoe style choice decision. The robots can not replace human shoe salesperson to make shoe style choice judgement more easily. They must need longer time to analyze whether which shoe style may be the most suitable to the shoe buyer. Otherwise, human shoe salesperson may attempt to make the most right shoe style choice decision to help any one shoe buyer to chooce the most right style shoe because he/she owns shoe style sale experience, shoe style knowledge, the most important reason is that they can feel every shoe customer individual emotion to touch whether he/she will feel comfortable or happy when they attempt to help every shoe customer to seek the most right shoe style in every shoe customer whole shoe searching processing. Othwerwise, serving robots are only one machine, they can not touch or feel every shoe customer individual emotion whether he/she feel comfortable or unhappy or happy when they need to contact them in whole shoe searching processing. Hence, I believe that some tasks robots can not repalce human staff to do very easily. Otherwise, robots may bring disadvanatges to let any one businessman to loss his/her customers, due to robots can not touch every customer

emotion to compare human staff in service tasks more easily. Robots serving customer behaviors may cause money lose and customers number lose to the shop in micro economic view.

On conclusion, in demand and supply economic theory for robots supply and demand case, robots supply number increasing may influence human workers demand number decrease. So, it seems that robots number supply will be depended on global robots supply number more than robots demand number because when human began to accept robots to replace human to do general simple jobs in global labor market. Then, it means that global robots labor number must need to be increased in order to satisfy global businessmen workers number need. If any kinds of robot workers manufacture number is not enough to be supplied to let global future businessmen to buy, then robot supply will be shortage and they can not provide to satisfy global businessmen robots labour purchase need. So, future robot number will be depended on supply more than demand.

Chapter 3 Human intellectual demand and supply behavior relationship
   Intellectual human economic behaviors
What does intellectual human economic behaviors mean ? Human foolish behavior is depended on social enjoyment need more or material social supply more? I believe that when we choose or decide to do intellectual behaviors, then our societies will be influenced to bring economic growth in consequence.I shall attempt to indicate pollution case to explain how and why eithet our intellectual or foolish behaviors may bring economic growth or recession in consequence as below:
On one hand, for air pollution social case aspect example, if we only consider to buy cars to drive for working aim or holiday leisure aim. Then, our societies air will be polluted. Our health will be influenced to bad. Our car driving behaviors may cause global environment air pollution serously. In long tiem, global air pollution will bring our bodies health to be bad. Although, ourselves car driving behaviors may bring our driving travelling leisure enjoyment and comfortable feeling in short time, also we so not need to pay public transport fare often, but we need to compensate ourselves health economic intangible loss due to air pollution , when cars number

increases, dirty air will cause ouselves health to become bad.

In the result, we will need to pay more medical expenditure when we are old age, due to ourselves bodies will become bad, due to we breathe global dirty air every day, due to ourselves cars pollute air in long time, e.g. 10 to 20 years, even 30 more without limited air pollution environment. So, driving cars behavior may be one kind of human foolish behavior and our foolish behavior may bring ourselves future long time medical expenditure absolutely.

One the other hand, water pollution social aspect, if we often keep much rubblish to pollute sea, oil exploration porcessing pollute ocean , ships gas pollute ocaen, then fishes will eat polluted food and drive dirty water, due to global ocean is polluted.

In fact, because human only to conside how to buy boats to carry on leisure enjoyment activities, or catch cruises to travel on the sea. Also, oil manufacturers only consider researching anywhere to find new oil exploration places to manufacture oil product, when their oil exploration processes pollute ocarn . Consequently, global fishes drink polluted warer or eat polluted food. They will have poison. SO, human will have high chance to eat poison polluted fishes, due to fishes are poison or are polluted. So, human is doing foolish activities, we only hope to find oil exploration places to pollute ocean or we only spend money to buy ticket to catch ships to travel anywhere in global ocean. All of these human foolish behaviors will bring pollution to global ocean. On consequently, we will need to compensate to eat polluted or dirty or poision fishes, ourselves bodies health will be bad. In long time, we need have high chance to pay medical expenditure when we are old. So, pollution case may be one good example to explain how and why human foolish behavior may influence ourselves future need to compensate serious medical loss.

All of these human foolish behavior will bring pollution to global ocean. On consequently, we will need to compensate to eat polluted or dirty or poison fished , ourselves bodies health will be bad. In long time, we will have high chance to pay medical expenditure, when we are old. So, pollution case may be one good example to explain how and why human ourselves intellectual or foolish behaviors may influence future long time economic loss or economic growth or recession in micro and micro economic view.

On another water pollution aspect hand, if we often keep rubbish to sea, oil exploration processing pollutes ocean and ships' gas pollute ocean, then fishes will eat polluted food and drink dirty water, due to fishes will eat polluted food and drink dirty sea water because the global ocean is polluted seriously.

In fact, because human only consider how to buy boats to carry on any leisure water activities, or catches cruises to travel on the sea. Also, oil manufacturers only consider any where to find oil exploratin places to manufacture oil products from ocean, when their pol exploration processes can plooute ocean. Consequently, global fishes drink polluted water or eat direty food. They will have poison. So, human will have high chance to eat poison fishes.

Otherwise, such as pollutin case, it can infuence inflation or deflation. Consequently, the reason indicates supply and demand theory. If air pollution is serious, then we will consider health issue, global cars demand number may be influenced to reduce, when global cars number demand will reduce, global car prices and supply number will need to change to fall down in order to attract or persuade global car consumers choose to make car purchase decision.

Hence, global car manufacture number and car price will be influenced to reduce, due to global air pollution issue. Consequently, deflation will occur because when the country citizen usually does not spend much extra saving money to buy car expensive goods. Money value will be low. Otherwise, if global cair pollution is not serious, human considers to buy cars to enjoy driving leisure lives. So, global car demand is influenced to increase , also global car price will also influenced to increase.

Consequently, gobal human will choose to buy cars to drive. Due to we accept to spend extra saving to buy expensive car goods. Car sale price and supply may be influenced to rise up. Money value is influenced to reduce. Inflation may be influenced, due to global car consumers number increases, we would not have extra money to spend easily. Car expensive goods expenditure influences our spending habit to avoid to make car purchase decision more easily. So, human intellectual or foolish activities may bring inflation or deflation consequency in possible indirectly in macro economic view.

On conclusion, above pollution case explain that how and why human intellectual or foolish economic behaviors may bring inflation or deflation consequency as wll as economic growth or recession consequency as well as any goods demand and supply increasing or decreasing consequency. It implies that human behavior may have indirect relationship to influence any goods demand and supply number to either increase or decrease result as well as any goods price will be influenced to increase or decrease in micro and macro economic view. Hence, Human foolish behavior is depended on social enjoyment need more or material social supply more because human needs to raise enjoyment feel , so we will choose to do foolish behavior, e.g. air pollution, when many people choose to buy cars to drive to replace catch public transport. So, such as car market, it depends on car demand number more than car supply number absolutely in demand and supply view.

The relationship between social change and human behavior

Why does economic changes may influence human individual behavioral change? I shall attempt to indicate shopping behavior and staying at home behavior to explain their case and effect relationsip as below:

Human behavior can be influenced by economic change or economic change can be influenced by human behavior? Why does recession may influence consumers reduce shopping desire? In social recession suitation, it is possible that many people lose jobs suddenly, due to businessmen lose many customers. They need to make decision to reduce employees number in order to continue to keep businesses. Consequently, many firms (organizations) their employees may lose jobs. When they have much time, due to lose jobs, they will feel to avoid to spend too much time and money to go to shopping often. Many losing jobs people, they will often stay at homes. So, they will reduce time to go to shopping, then non essential products won't their preferable choice purchase products. Hence, recession will change many losing jobs people their shopping or consumption desires to avoid to buy non essential products often . Usually when economic boom, many people have jobs to do because consumers number must increase when many people have jobs to do. Then, many people can accept to spend money to buy non essential products often. Many people feel spend time to go to shopping can satisfy their purchase of any kinds of new products useful psychology or desire. So, recession is one good example to explain it can influence many people do not like often to leave homes to go to shopping easily. Many people like to stay at homes, becaue they feel worry about spending too much shopping time when they leave homes. Their staying home time is one good negative shopping behavior example. So, economic change may influence human individual behavior changes , they have direct cause and efect relationship in behavioral economic view.

May human behavior influence economic change? Is it possible that human behavior may bring the country social economic change in macro economic or micro behavioral economic view ? I shall indicate publishing industry example. Do you feel that if there are many students feel learning is very important when they read many books or many of students feel interesting to read or they have reading new books in habit, then it is possible that the country will have many students like to spend time to go to any book shops to choose the books, they feel that they can help they learn new knowledge. Then the country will increase students number, they often spend time to visit any one book shop every week. Their visiting book shops behavior which may become their habits. So, the country will increase students number, they often spend time to visit book shops. Also, it implies that visiting book shops behaviors may be their behavioral habits.

So, when the country has many students often spend time to visit book shops , their visiting book shops behaviors may help any one book shop to raise books sale chance. So, the country's student individual often visiting book shop behaviors, their habitual visiting book shops behaviors must may assist help any one book shop to increase books sale number absolutely.

Consequently, any one book shop , its books sale bumber must be influenced to increase to increase because the country will have many students like or feel need visit book shops habit in order to choose any suitable books to buy to read at home in order to raise themselves learning effort. When the country has many bok shops often have many students visit their book shops, then their books sale number may be influenced to increase. It explain why student individual visiting book shop behavior may help any one book shop sale number increases also. So, visiting shops products sale number is depended on online products supply number, if online products supply number increases, then it may cause many customers choose to buy the kind of products from online webstore. So, any shop products sale number will depend on onlint products supply number in supply and demand view.

Human intellectual demand and supply behavior relationship

Human Behavioral network job brings social economic benefits

What does human network job mean ? Why may human network job be popular? Why human network job behavior may influence economy ?
Nowadays internet is popular to use. We can apply internet to find data , search any new things, even earn money. Why does internet
may become huma network job source. For example, e-publish may be one kind of new human network job. Any authors may apply internet
channel to help them to sell electronic or paper books from e-publisher web store. They may apply facebook, you tub etc. any online
channel to promote themselves new books to let new readers to know whether when they may buy themselves favourable new topic books to read from electronic publisher web store.

Thus, future electronic publisher industry may help any authors to build internet network platform to help them to sell and promote
ot advertise their any one new electronic or paper book topic to let global any one reader to choose to buy their any new topic books from electronic publisher web store easily and conveniently. However, it implies that electronic network platform author may be one kind of future new human network job in our societies.

How electronic network platform author job may bring economy benefit in macro economy view? A person can have few friends, contacts and still

be very influential if these few
friends and contacts are themselves highly influential, e.g. one author must not need to know any one reader in global society. When they like to choose any electronic books from electronic internet network platform. They may become the author's any one topic book buyer, when they feel the author's any one topic book is fun and attract they make decision to buth the strange author whose the topic book from electronic book publisher's platform web store conventiently in short time. Although, they are strangers, they do not know themselves , but the reader can understand what it way that made Google from writing platofrm to create new creative mind and typing network job method to replace traditional hand writing book method for global authors. It will be one kind of new human network writing job.

Hence, global any one reader can apply an innovative search engine , such as google.com to find whether whom author personal new topic books are value to read from internet.
Then, the electroniuc publisher's web store may be new book store platform sale network to help the author to sell many electronic or paper books from electronic network platform
in short time. So, internet may be future new network plaform to help global any one author to create network writing job absolutely. Furthermore, internet may be popular social media
to help any one author to build goold relationship between his/her readers. It is one kind of new network, human network job. New authors do not need to buy many paper books to prepare to put in any one book shop warehouse. Their every book can print on demand to reduce out of book stock in any one book shop. They may choose to sell either electronic books or paper books both from any one book publisher web store. So, electronic network platform may be one kind of good writing channel to help human authors to create income and it can also help authors to bring new creative mind and new topic fun content books to let readers to know and buy to read from electronic publisher network platform.

Why does human behavior may be one kind of new human network job to bring global economic advantages. ALthough, it may be free income or without inocme, but the person does the network behavior, his/her behavior may be bring advantages to influence many other people's health. For this case, when a worker in a coffee shop in an airport gets a vaccination againnst the flu, it does not only helps him or her stay healthy, but also helps the many travellers who might otherwise have been inflected if that workers caught the flu. So, the externality , the result implies the vaccination of even a part of a community conveys benefits to the whole community. For example, governments pay special attention to the vaccinations of school children, teachers, health mothers, and the elderly, categories of people particularly susceptible not only to catching, but also to transmitting a disease.

It is not accidential that governments are heavily involved with vaccination . When there are externalities, free market, fail to persuade individual incentives with society's

their the worker's decision of whether to get a vaccine ends up attracting whether other people get sick. The workers might not fully take all these other people's potential suffering into account when making her or his vaccination decision.

As Stanford University does many suggestions, understand this and tries to help them make the right decisions and so providers free flu vaccines for its staff and students.

Small pockets of unvaccinated individuals can allow a disease to gain a spread more widely well-being. For example, parent weighing the costs and benefits of a vaccine for their child is not always thinking of the consequences of that vaccination to other people. THese are markets in which subsidizing or regulating behavior can make everyone better off. Because the reason for requiring that a child be vaccinated before enrolling in school is not just to protect that child, because each child's vaccination affects others via potential contagions.

Robots take our jobs behavioral and economy influences

Robot job behavior brings economy influences

If one day robots can replace human to do simple, even complex jobs. They will bring what influences to our global societial economy.The popular economic refrain declares that the

global middle class is dying and robots will soon take our jobs, e.g. shopping center customer service jobs, library service jobs, cinema ticket sale jobs, restaurant kitchen cooker jobs,

even, bus drivers, taxi drivers etc. public transport driving jobs, accountant, doctors etc. professional jobs. Whether it is beautiful or petty matter if our future societies have many human jobs can be replaced to do from robots. Businessman must may reduce to employ employees and reduce to pay salary or wage, when robots can be replaced to do their employees tasks.

But, societies must bring unemployement rate rises , due to societies will have many people loss jobs when their employers choose to buy robots to serve their clients or do any office tasks or customer service or cleaning etc. tasks.

In micro economy view, employers may save money in long term, but in macro economy view, it will cause unemployment ratio rises , even crime rate rises when there are many people lose

jobs in societies. These models of doom, though, fail to account for the hundreds of businesses riding the waves of change in their industries when robots may be invented to replace human to do many simple , even complex tasks in our future societies.

WE may image that one small factory needs to manufacture fishes canes to sell to supermarket, the small , cheaper stuff and higher margin parts of the fishes manufacture industry. Before, this factory needs to employe many human factory workers need to help every fresh customer makeing the perfect fishing gear, designed for performance, durability, and cost in order to achieve to manufacture every fish cane in whole fished processing manufacturing stages. Every worker needs to spend about 15 to twenty minutes to finish every fish cane , till to delivery to any supermarket to sell. If this fish canes manufacturing factory can apply manufacturing robots to help them to finish any one working tasks , every robot can only spend five minutes to finish whole fresh fish cane manufacturing process. Thus, every robot can

help this factory save 10 to 15 minutes time to finsh every fish cane manufacturing process. IN fact, time is money, because when every robot can help this factory to reduce 10 to 15 minutes time to compare human worker. Then, this factory can finish about 20 fish canes in one hour if it can use robot to help it to manufacture fish canes. Otherwise, if this factory still use human workers to help it to manufacture fish canes, then it can finsh about 3 to 4 fish canes in one hour. SO, the manufacturing efficiency ensures that robots must help this fish manufacturing factory to raise fish canes number more than human workers. So, in robotic behavioral economy view, manufacturing robots must help this fish canes manufacturing factory to raise fish canes manufacturing number and deliver increasing number to supermarkets to prepare to sell every day. Robots can help this fish canes manufacturing factory bring manufacturing time saving, rising manufacturing efficiency, improving performance and reducing wages expenditure long time advantages in micro economy view. However, manufacturing robots can also bring disadvanages to society, e.g. increasing unemployment ratio, increasing crime rate,

this factory workers will lose jobs and income, they need earn social welfare from government and increasing government finance pressure in short time, even long time in macro economic view.

Stanford University graduate program in economics, Scott lecturer explained that "in demand and supply economic theory for robots supply and demand case, robots supply number increasing may influence human workers demand number decrease. It sometimes calls " the efficient frontier".

No specific human beings were mentioned in any of economics classes. As robots supply and demand in market case, They (robots) may be purely theoretical " agents" who reached to the most reasonable sale prices in order to persuade any one businessman buyer to make manufacturing robot buying decision whether robots can help him / her to bring how much saving time , saving money, saving cost, improving performance, efficiency economic benefit before he/she plans to reduce workers number when he/ she decides to apply robots to replace human workers in his/her factory or office or any service department, e.g. cinema ticket sale service, shopping center customer service, shopping center cleaning , supermarket customer service etc. service or sale tasks. When robots can replace human to do any one of these tasks in any organizations. So, robots may be human worker agents who reached to prices the way robots would react to a software

command. There was nothing that explained why some people thrived and others did n't or why truly brilliant, hardworking people could fail when much lazier folks succeeded." Having been admitted to the Stanford University graduate program in economics, Scott lecturer hoped to get his answers there.

How robots influence our future social changing? Using the right technology can be a boon to your business in this economy. For internet example, it is easier than ever to find well-matched customers all around the world, to stay in contact with them, and to more quickly design the products they want. If you focus solely on being cutting -edge, though you risk letting the technology

take over what should be very robust relationships with your customers , employees, and colleagues. IN nowaddays society, technoligical advances and cutomation, personal

relationships in business are more crucial than ever. I mean that robots can not replace human to serve clients to let them to feel more comfortable and passion more easily. For shoe shop case example, if the shoe shop apply one robot to serve its clients to replace human shoe salesperson to serve its shoe customers. Robots ensure that they can not persuade every shoe potential buyer to make shoe buying decision more easily when robots need to contact every shoe potential buyer. The reason is simple, because robots can not touch any one shoe buyer individual emotion very easier.

If the shoe buyer needs the robots to help him/her to choose any right shoe styles when he/she can not feel himself / herself can make the most right shoe style choice decision. The robots can not replace human shoe salesperson to make shoe style choice judgement more easily. They must need longer time to analyze whether which shoe style may be the most suitable to the shoe buyer. Otherwise, human shoe salesperson may attempt to make the most right shoe style choice decision to help any one shoe buyer to chooce the most right style shoe because he/she owns shoe style sale experience, shoe style knowledge, the most important reason is that they can feel every shoe customer individual emotion to touch whether he/she will feel comfortable or happy when they attempt to help every shoe customer to seek the most right shoe style in every shoe customer whole shoe searching processing. Othwerwise, serving robots are only one machine, they can not touch or feel every shoe customer individual emotion whether he/she feel comfortable or unhappy or happy when they need to contact them in whole shoe searching processing. Hence, I believe that some tasks robots can

not repalce human staff to do very easily. Otherwise, robots may bring disadvanatges to let any one businessman to loss his/her customers, due to robots can not touch every customer

emotion to compare human staff in service tasks more easily. Robots serving customer behaviors may cause money lose and customers number lose to the shop in micro economic view.

    Intellectual human economic behaviors

What does intellectual human economic behaviors mean ? I believe that when we choose or decide to do intellectual behaviors, then our societies will be influenced to bring economic growth in consequence.I shall attempt to indicate pollution case to explain how and why eithet our intellectual or foolish behaviors may bring economic growth or recession in consequence as below:

On one hand, for air pollution social case aspect example, if we only consider to buy cars to drive for working aimr or holiday leisure aim. Then, our societies air will be polluted. Our health will be influenced to bad. Our car driving behaviors may cause global environment air pollution serously. In long tiem, global air pollution will bring our bodies health to be bad. Although, ourselves car driving behaviors may bring our driving travelling leisure enjoyment and comfortable feeling in short time, also we so not need to pay public transport fare often, but we need to compensate ourselves health economic intangible loss due to air pollution , when cars number increases, dirty air will cause ouselves health to become bad.

In the result, we will need to pay more medical expenditure when we are old age, due to ourselves bodies will become bad, due to we breathe global dirty air every day, due to ourselves cars pollute air in long time, e.g. 10 to 20 years, even 30 more without limited air pollution environment. So, driving cars behavior may be one kind of human foolish behavior and our foolish behavior may bring ourselves future long time medical expenditure absolutely.

One the other hand, water pollution social aspect, if we often keep much rubblish to pollute sea, oil exploration porcessing pollute ocean , ships gas pollute ocaen, then fishes will eat polluted food and drive dirty water, due to global ocean is polluted.

In fact, because human only to conside how to buy boats to carry on leisure enjoyment activities, or catch cruises to travel on the sea. Also, oil manufacturers only consider researching anywhere to find new oil exploration places to manufacture oil product, when their oil exploration processes pollute ocarn . Consequently, global fishes drink polluted warer or eat polluted food. They will have poison. SO, human will have high chance to eat poison polluted fishes, due to fishes are poison or are polluted. So, human is doing foolish activities, we only hope to find oil exploration places to pollute ocean or we only spend money to buy ticket to catch ships to travel anywhere in global ocean. All of these human foolish behaviors will bring pollution to global ocean. On consequently, we will need to compensate to eat polluted or dirty or poision fishes, ourselves bodies health will be bad. In long time, we need have high chance to pay medical expenditure when we are old. So, pollution case may be one good example to explain how and why human foolish behavior may influence ourselves future need to compensate serious medical loss.

All of these human foolish behavior will bring pollution to global ocean. On consequently, we will need to compensate to eat polluted or dirty or poison fished , ourselves bodies health will be bad. In long time, we will have high chance to pay medical expenditure, when we are old. So, pollution case may be one good example to explain how and why human ourselves intellectual or foolish behaviors may influence future long time economic loss or economic growth or recession in micro and micro economic view.

On another water pollution aspect hand, if we often keep rubbish to sea, oil exploration processing pollutes ocean and ships' gas pollute ocean, then fishes will eat polluted food and drink dirty water, due to fishes will eat polluted food and drink dirty sea water because the global ocean is polluted seriously.

In fact, because human only consider how to buy boats to carry on any leisure water activities, or catches cruises to travel on the sea. Also, oil manufacturers only consider any where to find oil exploratin places to manufacture oil products from ocean, when their pol exploration processes can plooute ocean. Consequently, global fishes drink polluted water or eat direty food. They will have poison. So, human will have high chance to eat poison fishes.

Otherwise, such as pollutin case, it can infuence inflation or deflation. Consequently, the reason indicates supply and demand theory. If air pollution is serious, then we will consider health issue, global cars demand number may be influenced to reduce, when global cars number demand will reduce, global car prices and supply number will need to change to fall down in order to attract or persuade global car consumers choose to make car purchase decision.

Hence, global car manufacture number and car price will be influenced to reduce, due to global air pollution issue. Consequently, deflation will occur because when the country citizen usually does not spend much extra saving money to buy car expensive goods. Money value will be low. Otherwise, if global cair pollution is not serious, human considers to buy cars to enjoy driving leisure lives. So, global car demand is influenced to increase , also global car price will also influenced to increase.

Consequently, gobal human will choose to buy cars to drive. Due to we accept to spend extra saving to buy expensive car goods. Car sale price and supply may be influenced to rise up. Money value is influenced to reduce. Inflation may be influenced, due to global car consumers number increases, we would not have extra money to spend easily. Car expensive goods expenditure influences our spending habit to avoid to make car purchase decision more easily. So, human intellectual or foolish activities may bring inflation or deflation consequency in possible indirectly in macro economic view.

On conclusion, above pollution case explain that how and why human intellectual or foolish economic behaviors may bring inflation or deflation consequency as wll as economic growth or recession consequency as well as any goods demand and supply increasing or decreasing consequency. It implies that human behavior may have indirect relationship to influence any goods demand and supply number to either increase or decrease result as well as any goods price will be influenced to increase or decrease in micro and macro economic view.

The relationship between social change and human behavior

Why does economic changes may influence human individual behavioral change? I shall attempt to indicate shopping behavior and staying at home behavior to explain their case and effect relationsip as below:

Human behavior can be influenced by economic change or economic change can be influenced by human behavior? Why does recession may influence consumers reduce shopping desire? In social recession suitation, it is possible that many people lose jobs suddenly, due to businessmen lose many customers. They need to make decision to reduce employees number in order to continue to keep businesses. Consequently, many firms (organizations) their employees may lose jobs. When they have much time, due to lose jobs, they will feel to avoid to spend too much time and money to go to shopping often. Many losing jobs people, they will often stay at homes. So, they will reduce time to go to shopping, then non essential products won't their preferable choice purchase products. Hence, recession will change many losing jobs people their shopping or consumption desires to avoid to buy non essential products often . Usually when economic boom, many people have jobs to do because consumers number must increase when many people have jobs to do. Then, many people can accept to spend money to buy non essential products often. Many people feel spend time to go to shopping can satisfy their purchase of any kinds of new products useful psychology or desire. So, recession is one good example to explain it can influence many people do not like often to leave homes to go to shopping easily. Many people like to stay at homes, becaue they feel worry about spending too much shopping time when they leave homes. Their staying home time is one good negative shopping behavior example. So, economic change may influence human individual behavior changes , they have direct cause and efect relationship in behavioral economic view.

May human behavior influence economic change? Is it possible that human behavior may bring the country social economic change in macro economic or micro behavioral economic view ? I shall indicate publishing industry example. Do you feel that if there are many students feel learning is very important when they read many books or many of students feel interesting to read or they have reading new books in habit, then it is possible that the country will have many students like to spend time to go to any book shops to choose the books, they feel that they can help they learn new knowledge. Then the country will increase students number, they often spend time to visit any one book shop every week. Their visiting book shops behavior which may become their habits. So, the country will increase students number, they often spend time to visit book shops. Also, it implies that visiting book shops behaviors may be their behavioral habits.

So, when the country has many students often spend time to visit book shops , their visiting book shops behaviors may help any one book shop to raise books sale chance. So, the country's student individual often visiting book shop behaviors, their habitual visiting book shops behaviors must may assist help any one book shop to increase books sale number absolutely.

Consequently, any one book shop , its books sale bumber must be influenced to increase to increase because the country will have many students like or feel need visit book shops habit in order to choose any suitable books to buy to read at home in order to raise themselves learning effort. When the country has many bok shops often have many students visit their book shops, then their books sale number may be influenced to increase. It explain why student individual visiting book shop behavior may help any one book shop sale number increases also.

How human productive behavior may influence economic development

May any country which citizen behavior assist themselves country development? It is one cause and effect economic question. I mean that if the country itself citicen can not concentrate mind or energy to choose to do one kind of industry in order to let themselves country can bring the most benefit, then whether the counry itself economy can bring the most serious economic benefit. I shall attempt to indicate these countries themselves indistry choice to explain whether these countries themselves citizen productive behavior may help themselves countries to achieve the largest economic benefits. I shall indicate as below:

New Zealand farmer individual wine productive behavior

For New Zealand country example, this country concerns itself effort is foucs on farming agricultural aspect. So, this country has many farmers concentrate on farming agricultural aspect. May New Zealanders choose to spend time to produce different kinds of wines, e.g. wine or red grape wine is for the people are eating meat, or they are eating dinner.

When these New Zealanders their behaviors choose to do farming or agriculture to grow and produce different kinds of taste of white or red grape wine drinking products job. Themselves grape agriculture behavior will influence these New Zealanders themselves, they can learn how to improve different kinds of grape wine drinking products in order to achieve every kinds of white or read grape wines taste improving aim during their white or red grape producing process.

Why can New Zealander every individual white or read grape wine producers improve their white or read grape wine taste more easily? In behavioral economic view, it can explain that why any one New Zealander white or read grape wine producer can be encouraged or excited or persuaded to concentrate nervous and energy and effort to learn how to improve their white or red grape wine products easily.

In fact, New Zealand is one agricultural food export country. It has good natural environment resource , e.g. land, seed to provide any one farmer to produce themselves any kinds of agricultrual food products, e.g. fruit, or wine food products. Because New Zealanders know themselves country has enough natural resource . So, in common, many New Zealanders choose to attempt to do farming agricultural jobs in order to export themselves any kinds of fruit or meat or wine products to overseas or sell to domestic in order to earn profit.

So, when these New Zealand farmers number has been increasing every year. This country farmers will feel themsleves competition between this New Zealand farmers themselves are serious due to they may feel New Zealanders choose to do agriculture businesses in order to export themselves different kinds of farming food to overseas or sell to local to earn profit.

Hence, when many New Zealand farmers feel that farmers number has been increasing every year. They will feel themselves competition is serious. They must need to spend much time and nervous and effort to research what method is the best how to produce the best taste of white or red grape wine products in order to let local or overseas wine buyers to choose to buy his/her producing white or read grpae products to drink.

Hence, in competition psychological view, may influence many New

Zealand white or reaad wine producers had been beginning to change their learning behavior on researching what method is the best in order to produce the best quality of taste red or white wine products to sell in order to attract overseas or local white or read grape wine drinkers to choose to buy his/her wine products. Their behavior will focus on learning how to raising or improving white or read grape wine taste method more than only focus on producing a large number white or red grape wine products. They believe wine quality is more important to compare wine producing number. So, New Zealand wine producers themselves wine producers behaviors have been changing on concentrating on researching wine quality method aspect more then wine producing number aspect in behavioral economic view.

America high technological productive behavior

For America example, US is one high technological country, it owns many high technological knowledge talent inventors, e.g. computer science inventors. Hence, US must attract many diferent countries owning high technological computer inventors choose to go to US to develop their computer science profession career. Also, it seems that when many computer science inventors or professions choose to go to US to develop themselves computer science new career. In behavioral economic view, due to their leaving themselves countries choice, which may bring influence themselve country job behaviors need to be changed. They must need to adapt US new live. Because they will forgive their past computer science job. These computer science professionals need to spend time to adapt US new lives. They " past computer science job behaviors" will need to be changed to their new US any computer employer's new computer science job model.

Because their traditional computer science jobs needed to be forgot in their themselves countries. They will feel their old computer science job knowledge and behavior needed to change in order to let their US any one new of computer company employer feels satisfactory to accept their new working behavior in any one US computer organization.

So, on the other hand, many US computer company employer will feel that they must need time to accept any one new overseas computer science professions their working behaviors, their working attitude daily, because these foreign comouter science professional, their past computer working behaviors and working attitude must be different to US domestic computer science professions.

In behavioral economic view, these overseas computer science professions, their working behaviors and attitude must be needed to change in order to adapt any one US new computer company itself domestic or local computer science professional stafs themselves daily working behaviors and attitude because these overseas and local computer science professionals must need to team work together.

In behavioral economic view, it is only one way that foreign computer science professionals must need to change themselves past country traditiona daily working behaviors and attitude in order to cooperate with these US local computer science professionals in teams more easily.

Consequently, if these foreign compute science professionals can change their past working behaviors and attitude to let any one US local computer science professional feels to cooperate with them easily in short time. Then, the US computer company itself whole computer professional teams themselves efficiencies will be influenced to raised or improved by the changing past working attitude and working behaviors of these foreign computer science professionals. So, in behavioral economic view, only if US any one computer company hopes itself computer teams themselves efficiency can be raised or improved when it decides to employ foreign computer science professionals and US domestic computer science professionals. They need to work in teams together. They must need to let these foreign computer science professionals to know how to change their working behaviors and attitude to let their domestic computer science professionals feel easy to work together. Then, the US computer company itself whole team efficiency must be rasied or improved easily in short time.

● China share market investing behavior

For China share market example, economic development depends on financial market. Because if many Chinese have interest to invest to carry on shares buying and selling activities in orde to learn how to earn shares interest and share profit when the China shareholder can make decision to sell himself/herself shares in the the high price, then he/she can earn money when he/she can sell the China company's shares in the high sale share price position.

If China has many Chinese like to spend time to carry on investing shares activities. Themselves shares buying and selling behaviors will influence China has many companies can increase fund from many Chinese shareholders in order to have enough money to expand or develop themselves businesses in China in long term.

Consequently, when China can have many Chinese like to attempt to carry on buying and selling shares investing behaviors in China share market. Themselves buying and selling shares behaviors can help many Chinese companies have effort to increase enough money or capital in order to continue to do their businesses in long term absolutely. So, it explains why when many Chinese become shareholders , they can assist China will have many companies continue to develop their businesses if many Chinese like to carry on shares buying and selling investing behaviors in long time in China financial investment market nowadays in behavioral economic view.

Why has any individual country have many people invest share behavior which can influence the country's macro consumption desire?

I shall apply shares market buying and selling investment behavior to explaiin why shares investment behavior which may impact the country's overal consumption desire as below:

In behavioral economic view, I assume that when the coutry has many people have interest to attempt to carry on shares buying and selling investment behavior, then their frequent shares buying and selling behaviors which may bring negactive consumption desire or shopping desire of these shares investors their consumer behavior.

The reason is simple, when the country has many share buyers number suddenly been increasing rapidly. Consequently, these large group share investors must need to spend much time to research any kinds of company shares variations, whether when their share prices will rise up of fall down in order to achieve buying the company's shares in the lowest price and selling the company's shares in the highest price level in order to earn profit.

Basic on this reason, they must need to spend much extra time to research share prices changing behavior every day, e.g. one working person will wait to leave his/her job, after he/she can spend time to gather data to research the day's share price changing behavior after dinner. So, the working person's right time may be his/her share price market research behavior. Before he/she may spend his/her night time to go to shopping after dinner, but nowadays, he/she will fogive to do his/her shopping behavior before dinner or after dinner at hight sometime. He/she will make decision to spend much night time to turn on computer to click on share market website to research his/her share purchase choice to investigate whether his/her share price whether it rises up or falls down at the moment in order to make his/her share buying or selling decision at ever night time.

I mean the when the country has many people are share investors, their shares investment behavioral spenging time which will influence many shops lose customers at might often because the country will have many people feel need to spend night time to turn on computer or watch television to investigate share price variation. So, the country will have many people / share investors choose to stay at home in order to carry on share price variation investigation behavior, they need to listen share market update news from radios or watch the share market update news from computer or TV at home every night. Consequenly, they must reduce times to leave themselves homes at night. So, their shopping behavior also will be reduced. Because these share investors feel need to spend time to investigate share price variation news at homes which can bring economic benefits (high opportunity benefits) when they choose to forgive to leave homes to go to shopping times (opportunity cost) every night.

On conclusion, it seems that when the country has many people are share investors, then their share price investigating behavior may bring negative shopping emotion at night. Consequently, the country's any one shop may lose many customers from this share investor consumer group in behavioral economic view. Hence, when the country's share investors number had been increasing rapidly, it will influence any shops lose many customers from this share investing customer group at night frequenly in short time, even long time in behavioral economic view, because their shopping desires or shopping emotion will be brought negative feeling when they make decisions to spend much time to listen radios or watch TV or computers share price update nes at night. Hence, share market will bring negative impact to influence consumer shopping desire or negative shopping emotion in behavioral economic view.

Can technology influence human shopping behavioral change?
Nowadays, technological development has reached mature stage, whether technological mature stage may bring positive or negative shopping emotion influence to global consumers. I shall aplly internet inventin or ecommerce shopping channel tool to explain whether internet technology can bring postive or negative influence to global consumer behavior in behavioral economic view.
Internet is a good technological tool, it brings e-commerce business chance. In fact, commonly, global has have many businessmen choose to use internet channel to carry on their products transactions between global

online-buyers and their electronic websites. So, global many shoppers had begun to feel online shopping is more convenient to compare visiting shops shopping. Their shopping behaviors have been changed from internet technological tool. Global has many shoppers choose to buy any products from any overseas or local businessmen their web stores. They only need to spend time to find any businessmen their webstores to choose the most suitable products to pay visa to buy from their webstores. at homes. So, in general, global had have may shoppers had changed their shopping behaviors from visiting shops to visiting webstores at homes often.

So, it seems that internet technological tool had influenced global many shops disappear, but internet webstores will be replaced their actual shops on streets. Some of businessmen either they choose webstores to replace shops or choose websotes and shops both or still keep shops only. Hence, internet tool influences global businessmen have three kinds of products sale channels to let globa local and overseas consumers to choose how to buy their products.

However, in fact, many of global shoppers, youngers and olders had begun to accept to buy any products from webstores. They feel to spend time to leave homes to visit shops , their shopping behaviors will be wasted time to not essential part to their daily lives. Hence, since internet technological invention, it had changed many consumers their traditional visiting shops shopping habit to change to buying products from webstores channel.

However, on the one hand, internet creates webstores ecommerce shopping channel to let global many consumers do not need to leave homes to go to shopping. It brings negative visiting shops shopping emotion to global general consumers nowadays. But on the other hand, it also brings positive visiting internet webstores shopping emotion to global general consumer nowadays. So, it seems that global many consumers feel that they often do not need to spend much time to go out shopping. Many global consumers feel convenient and enjoy to choose any products to buy from different internet webstores, when the online buyer chooses the most suitable product, he she only needs to pay visa card to buy the product from the online seller's webstore conveniently at home.

Hence, online shopping can bring economic benefit to online buyers, e.g. avoiding walking time or spending transport fare to visit the shop to go to shopping, shortening or reducing shopping time to do another important matter.

On conclusion, global many consumers began feel online shopping can bring more economic benefits on shortening shopping time, avoiding transport fare spending aspect. So, online shopping will be popular shopping behavior for future long time. It may encourage global many shoppers can make rapid shopping decision in short time in order to carry on any products buying transaction to global any one online shopper in short time easily in behavioral economic view. So, global many businessmen had begun to build themselves one attraction webstore in order to persuade different countries consumers to choose to click themselves webstores from internet channel to buy any kinds of products in short time easily.

So, internet technology had changed consumers traditional shopping behaviors to build positive online shopping emotion as well as raise online sellers' any products sale chance easily in behavioral economic view.

Why and how human behavior may influence the country's economic growth or recession?

When one country has many people choose to do the same matter for one period, whether their behavior may influence the country's pvera; economic growth or recession . I shall attempt to indicate cases toexplain their relationship as below:

For flowing rubblish behavioral case example, do you feel that when the country has many people often flow rubblish on the streets, instead of their flowing rubblish behavior may bring streets dirty? But, their flowing rubblish behavior may explain that this country has people may have enough money to buy food to ear, or enough cloths to wear, enough bottles of water to drink, even they may have enough money to buy new television, radio, refrigeraters , washing machines, desktops or laptops electronic home products from old to new to use in order to satisfy their living needs. So, when they flow old electronic home products, their flowing old home electronic products behaviors may seem that they have enough money to buy other new home electronic products to replace old home electronic products to use at homes.

However, it seems thaat this country ought have many people have jobs to do. So, many of them, they can easy to make purchase decison to flow any old home electronic products and buy any new home electronic products to use . Because this country has many people have jobs to do. So, they can often not use old home electonic products to become rubblishs to flow on streets after they had bought any kinds of new home electronic homes.

In fact, it also implies that this country's economy grows rapidly. So, many businesses can glow up rapdly. When they expanded their businesses, they must need to increase employees number in order to let they help themselves to raise productivity or serve their clients absolutely. So, when the country has many businesses can grow up, it seems that its economy must be better or it is improved to compare past. Due to many different kinds of home electronic products had been often bought to use by this country people in this period. So, this country's any streets can be observed that expensive electronic home products were flowed on streets anywhere. then, this country will have many electronic home products sellers can sell their home electronic products very easily. When this country has many people can find any kinds of jobs to do easily. So, due to unemploymen rate had been decreasing.

In behavioral economic view, as this many electronic home products rubblish country case, we can observe this country may have many people have jobs to do. So, consumption number has been increased long time. So, cheap food, or expensive home electronic products may be rubblish on any streets. This country's people , their flowing rubblish behaviors may be explained that many of people have enough jobs to do, so they have ability to buy any good taste food to eat or buy any kinds of expensive electronic home products to use. So, this country's economy may be improved for this long period. So, in behavioral economic view, when this country can have many electronic home products rubblishs are flowed on anywherer in streets frequently. It seems that this country will have many people have jobs to do, so it causes they often change old home electronic products or replaced them easily, when they have enough income to spend to buy any kinds of new home electronic products to use at homes easily. Moreover, their flowing old electronic home products behaviors also indicate that this country has many people their salaries may be increased in possible from their emplyers. When this country can have many different kinds of home electornic products are sold. It means that this country's electronic home products needs or demand had been increasing, due to many people have jobs to do and income increases to excite their living of needs also improve. Consequently, this country may seem have better economic improvement. We can observe from this country's electronic home products rubblish increasing income in theis period.

On conclusion, this country ought experience economic growth at this period. So, " flowing expensive electronic home rubblish increasing number " may seem that this country's economic growth is rapidly in this period, due to many people have jobs to do as well as salaries increase in this period.

Technology how impacts human behavior changing?

Technology how influences human behavior to bring changing? For example, online share purchase and sale transaction from smart phone brings share investor can do share buying or selling transation in any where and any time conveniently, non manual driving auto vehicle, bring car owner feels comfortable and spends free time to do other matter, e.g. reading, listening mucis in himself or herself car freely. electrical energy vehicle can help car owner to reduce air polluton and it can brings the drivers do not feel drive long time in any journeys in order to avoid air pollution for environmental protection responsible car drivers in our societies. Thus, they will drive long time in any journeys when they can drive electronic energy cars to replace oil energy cars.

However, online technology can also bring consumers can choose to stay at homes to buy any things from seller individual online webstore conveniently. Such as online technology can bring shoppers do not need to spend much time to visit shops to buy any things. They can choose any kinds of products from any online sellers individual online webstores conveniently at homes. Online technology excite busy consumers can make purchase decision easily as well as it can help online sellers sell any kinds of products from internet easily.

In behavioral economic view, technology can change human behavior to be improved, it can let human feels comfortable, more free time ro use, rapid making any decisions, such as apply smart phones to make share purchase or sale transaction decision, online shopping decision, even travelling any where decision in short time, when the traveller finds the most cheap hotel accommodation room price and air ticket price frm any travel agent online tourism webstore, then the potential travel customer can follow the online hotel accommodation price and air ticket price data to make decision when to buy the air ticket from the airline travel agent or make decision when to prebook which hotel accommodation room to go to the country to travel from online travel agent tourism webstores. So, technology can encourage global any country travelers to make anywhere to trvel rapidly. If the traveler can find the country's general hotel rooms and airline tickets prices had been decreasing more sightly. The traveler may make travel decision to choose the country to travel in short time, then he/she can prebook the country;s any hotel room and airline ticket to pay by visa fraom the country's any hotel and airline travel agent webstores., before one week, even one month or more easily. Hence, online technology can also encourage traveler individual frequent travel times to be increased, due to global travelers can find any hotel rooms and airline tickets prices from internet conveniently at homes. They do not need to spend time to visit any airline travel agent to enquire travel choice country's hotel rooms prices and airline ticket prices. They can compare global travel of countries choices ' all hotels rooms and airline agents air tickets prices to make prebook airline seat and hotel room decision before one week, one month even six months early.

On conclusion, online technology can encourage global travelers can make travelling any where and when traveling time desicions easily. It can excite tourism industry develops in long time. Also, such as electricity cars invention can encourage environment protection car owners do car purchase decision easily, because they can choose to drive electronic energy cars to replace oil energy cars in order to avoid air pollution occurs easily. So, electronic cars can increase electronic car purchasrs number, due to many of environmental protection attitude of car owners can choose to drive electricity cars to bring air cleans, even non -manual driving cars can encourage lazy driving and free time driving car owners to choose to buy non-manual (artificial intelligent) cars to drive , because they can spend much free time to read, listen music or do any matters in themselves cars, they do not need to drive cars, robotic (AI) auto driving machine is such one non-manual driver to help them to drive themselves cars confidently. So, non-manual driving cars can attract lazy and enjoying free time driving car owners to choose to buy to replace traditional manual cars to drive easily. Moreover, online share transaction can help any share investors to make share buying and selling decision in short time easily. When they can apply smart phones technological tool to carry on share buying and selling activities easily. They can observe any share rising or falling price suitation from smart phones in any where any any time easily. So, smart phone technology can help global any shareholders to make share purchase and sale transaction easily. So, technology can encourage human makes decision in short time rapidly.

How and why employees behaviors may influence economy development?

In behavioral economy view,I believe the country's any organizational employees behavior may bring indirect relationship to influence the country's long term economic development. I shall indicate past manufacture industry social development period to explain their relationship. For many countries' past business activities had belonged to manufacturing industry, such as US, UK past before 1980 year, it focused on steel manufacturing and steel manufacturing related machine products. So, US, Uk developed countries manufacturing industries may be past main country's economic income sources. I assume US , UK past had one million number different kinds of industries. They ought had about seven houndred thousand number organizational businesses were belonged to manufactured industry. They may include:

Steel manufacturing and steel related machine manufacturing, e.g. vehicle manufacturing, home appliances, e.g. washing machine, television, radio, refrigerate cooler, heater, air condition etc. different kinds of different kinds of steel -related manufacturing machine, they were manufactured from US, UK steel machine manufacturers. So, US, Uk the other three hundred thousand number industry may be general service industry, e.g. hotel service, restaurent, cinema, public transport service, tourism lesiure , wine bar, supermarket etc. different kinds of non-manufacturing industries business organizations were operated in UK, US past before 1980 year.

So, in UK, US developed countries industry development history, they ought have high percentage of businesses belonged to steel related manufacturing machine and steel products. Also, in the past before 1980 year, US, Uk business employers , they employed many workers are manufacturing workers. They needed to spend long time to work in factories. They were skillful workers, and they are trained to manufacturing cars, washing machine, television, heater, etc. even steel itself different kinds of steel related products to prepare to deliver to their shops to sell to US, Uk local or overseas clients.

So, I believe that past UK, US ought employ many employees, they belonged to skillful manufacturing workers, manufacture increasing steel machine or steel related machine number of products rapidly daily. So, if UK, US had had many of these manufacturing factories owned high skillful workers, then their manufacturing steel-related machine or steel both kinds of products number must be influenced to raise rapidly. Consequently, their steel machine manufacturing products would been exported to overseas or would been sold to local both markets , they may be influenced to raise sale number. They (these manufacturing workers) needed to be trained to know how to manufactur these different kinds of machine products in the efficient teams and they ought to be trained to raise their efficiencies in order to shorten time to manufacturing many kinds of steel related manufacturing machine or steel itself products rapidly. So , if their efficiencies and manufacturing performance was improved, these US, UK any one manufacturing worker and their teams ought achieve raising productivities significantly.

Hence, when past UK, US manufacturing industry development period, if these two countries' any manufacturing factories could have many manufacturing workers could be trained to be skillful and proficient manufacturing workers. Then, in past every day to these factories workers, they ought help their steel or steel related manufacturing employers to raise any kinds of machine or steel products number in every team. So, when past in the manufacturing industry development, US, UK could have many factories' manufacturing workers themselves steel or steel related machine products manufacturing skill could be trained to to improve to any kinds of these machine or steel manufacuring products quality as well as their products number could be influenced to raise by themselves skillful improvement significantly every day.

Then, what would be influenced to occur to past UK, US manufacturing industry period? In behavioral economic view, when these two manufacturing industry developed countries, such as UK, US , if they had many factories workers can be trained to improve their skill in order to achieve any kinds of steel or steel-related machine products quality could be improved as well as products manufacturing number could be also increased absolutely.

In consequence, past UK and US both countries ought increase themselves any kinds of steel and steel related machine products number to be supplied to themselves local shops to let local clients to choose any one kind of machine manufacturing products to buy easily as well as they could also export to supply overseas any countries to buy their different kinds of steel or steel related machine products to let overseas steel or steel related manufacturing machine product buyers, they can have many of these different kinds of these steel or steel-related different kinds of manufacturing machine from UK and UK these both countries easily to compare other countries.

On conclusion, I believe that past US, and UK macro manufacturing industry income GDP would increase significantly. So, they would have good economic growth performance because when many of these manufacturing workers themselves manufacturing effort could be improved. So, it explained when employees manufacturing abilities can influence economic growth indirectly.

Robots invention whether they can help organizations to raise efficiencies or inefficiencies?

In behavioral economic view, in any organizations, when the organization hopes its worker teams can raise efficiencies , the organization may choose to increase more workers number and/or it can provide training to improve these workets themselves skills in order to raise their efficiencies. For one warehouse example, when the warehouse increases many goods , they are needed to delivered these goods from the shelves to the delivering destination locations. If this warehouse supervisors feel these workers themselves goods delivery speeds are slow, which is possible due to this warehouse's workers number is not enough. So, this warehouse supervisor ought increase workers number in order to increase their goods delivery speed in order to deliver goods from the shelves to every indicated goods delivery destination in order to let any one lorry driver can transport the right kinds of goods and ensure the accurate goods number to transport to any one client home rapidly.

However, if this warehouse supervisor planed to buy several warehouse goods delivery robots to assist these warehouse workers to find the right kinds of goods from shelves and then deliver to the right destination location in the warehouse. So, these warehouse orkers can concentrate on counting the accurate goods number and ensuring the right kinds of goods in order to prepare to let lorry drivers to transport these goods to these goods of buyers themselvers homes rapidly. Consequently, in the first step, robots can concentrate on finding th right goods from shelves and delivers them to the right goods transportation of location destination. Then, in the second step, these warehouse workers can concentrate on counting the accurate goods number and ensuring the right kinds of goods in order to prepare to put them to the lorry. Consequently, when warehouse robots and warehouse workers can cooperate to work together, the most important, robots, can deal on finding the right kinds of goods and deal on delivering the accurate number of goods of job duty as well as these warehouse workers can only concentrte on counting the right kinds of goods number in order to avoid it has none any mistake of wrong kinds of goods and inaccurate goods of delivery number to be transported to the lorry and to deliver to any one buyer's home.

So, it seems that warehouse robots ought help any one warehouse worker to raise himself efficiency and avoid goods delivery of mistake occurrence easily as well as their help to warehouse workers that can let any one goods buyer feels their goods can be delivered to their homes rapidly. Moreover, warehouse robots can also help these warehouse workers to raise efficiencies because warehouse robots can help them to shorten goods delivery time between any one shelf and any one goods delivery destination of location in the warehuse because robots may help them to find the right kinds of goods from the right shelf in the short time. So, any one worker does not need to spend long time to seek anywhere is the right shelf location for the kind of goods when the kind of goods are needed to deliver to the buyer's home from lorry. Warehouse robots can help them to do this aspect of " finding the goods from the right shelf in short time job duty". So, any one warehouse worker only needed tospend less time to do the counting of any right kind of goods number and ensuring the right kind of goods job duty. Consequently, this warehouse 's any one worker, his any one kind of goods delivery time may be reduced, because robots' assistance and they may have more confidence to avoid mistake to deliver the wrong number of goods and/or the wrong kind of goods to any one goods buyer's home.

On conclusion, it seems that warehouse robots ought may help any one warehouse worker to raise efficiency for any one team in the warehouse as well as the warehouse any one supervisor does not need to spend much time to observe any one worker individual performance for " goods delivery job duty aspect" because their goods delivery job duty that had been replaced to do by these several warehouse robots. Robots can achieve the more accurate of right kinds of goods and the right number of goods delviery job performance to compare any one of human warehouse worker themselves right kinds of goods of delivery and right number of goods of delivery job performance. So, when robots can participate to cooperate with this warehouse's any one worker to do their goods of delivery job duty in this warehouse every day. Then, robots can raies any one of supervisor individual confidence in order to let they do not need to spend time to observe any one of worker individual whose goods of delivery job performane. They can concentrate on supervising any one worker whose goods transport to lorry in the final step in order to avoid to deliver wrong goods number and / or wrong kind of goods to any one goods buyer's home every day. Consequently, this warehouse's overall teams of their delviery of goods performance many be improved by robotss' participatin to goods of delivery task as well as this warehouse's oveall teams themselves efficiencies may be influenced to raise by robots' goods of delivery task participation.

Why social behavior may influence organizational strategy needs to be changed ?

Why any organizations need to know whether nowadays social behaivor how has been changing in order to implement the kind of the most right strategy to achieve the profit aim pursue in possible. I shall indicate nowadays ecommerce or online, customer shopping behavior to explain above question concerns they ought have close relationship between social behavior and organizational strategic choice or organizational behavioral changing need.

On nowadays ecommerce business, or online shopping model, this kind of shopping model in global many young and old age consumers like to apply internet tool to choose any country sellers website stores in order to stay at home to buy any kinds of products from themselves webstores in global societies.

In fact, online shopping model had been popular for long time above to twenty years. Most of global sellers will make decision to design themselves webstores in order to attract global many online buyers to choose to buy their products from themselves webstores. So, it seems that social consumers purchase behaviors had been changed to online shopping from internet invention.

Hence, social consumers purchase behavioral changes may influence any organizations' strategies need to be changed from visiting shops purchase strategy model to online purchase strategy model, if the seller still concentrate on concentrate on considerate how to design itelf , but neglects to considerate how to design itself webstore, e.g. how to design attract product photos to put on itself webstore, how to arrange sale price information location to be putted on webstore and visa card payment location on itself webstore in order to let any one online buyer can feel very easier to buy itself any kinds of products from itself webstore. Then, its potential online buyers will be influenced to increase number when they can find this online seller itself any kinds of products photes and every kinds of product sale price information and visa card payment channel locations easily from itself webstore.

So, it implies that nowadays any one seller ought need to design one webstore to let any one online overseas and domestic consumers can have chance to click itself webstore to choose any one kind of product to buy conveniently when he/she does not hope to leave him/her home to go to shop, because nowadays social shopping behaviors had been influenced to change when internet invention, them it gives another online purchase method to replace visiting shops purchase method to global any one buyer in nowadays societies.

So, if nowadays any one seller still concentrate on how to design itself shop display in order to put any kinds of product on shelf in order to let any one visiting shop customer to find the kind of product to buy, but it neglects to change to choose to pursue another new technological shopping method, such as webstore purchase method in order to implement effective strategy to design the most right webstore as well as in order to attract global overseas and local consumers to find itself webstore easily from website and find its any one kind of product phots and sale price and visa card payment button in order to choose to buy itself any kinds of products in the short time. Consequently I believe that the seller will lose many customers from overseas and local when its other same or similar product sellers choose to design themselves webstores in order to let global any one product buyer can buy themselves any one kind of product when they can pay visa card to buy their products from them webstores conveniently when they stay at home habily. Then, the seller will lose many global potential customers in long time.

On conclusion, in behavioral economic view, any consumer behavioral social changing, which will influence any in order to avoid customers number loses significantly . In future time, organizations need to make rapid decision in order to implement the most reasonable and the most useful strategy in order to avoid global potential customers number reduces or lose them in long time. So, social behavioral changing environment ought influence any global organizations need to decide how to change themselves strategies in order to avoid customers loses significantly in future time.

How and why human behavior may influence economic growth or recession?

May ourselves daily behaviors influence our global societial continue economic growth or recession? Do they have cause and effect close relationship between human behaviors and global economic growth or recession? I shall apply behavioral economic theory to analyze and explain whether ourselves daily behaviors and our global societial economic growth

or recession which have close cause and effect relationship as below:
Every country itself economic development must depend on any business activities, otherwise, any kinds of business activities must need ourselves business activities or behaviors in order to achieve any business activities as well as achieve the country's overall economic development in macro view. However, any country's overall business activites or behaviors which must depend on any kinds of individual businessmen, themselves employees daily working behavior or activity or performance in order to help them to attract or increase many clients number to acieve " earning profit" aim. So, it seems that any individual business, itself overall every department individual working behavior is one main factor to influence the company's overall business performance.

For agricultural fruit and meat food farming industry example, such as New Zealand is a farming main target industry country. It had had many New Zealanders were daily themselves own farming businesses for many years. Their farming businesses include growing fruit, sheep, cow, pig pork, meat etc. food sale business. If the New Zealand farmer owned a large size farming land, then he will choose either growing fruit or feeding sheeps, pigs, cows to be meat to to transport to New Zealand supermarkets to help them to sell to their farmers meet to New Zealanders in order to earn profit. Thus, if the New Zealand farmer owned large size of farming lands, then he needs to employ many farming employees (farming workers) to help him to carry on farming business daily tasks, e.g. picking up friuts, feeding pigs, cows, sheeps to eat food daily. These daily farming jobs are very important to influence this New Zealand farmer's meats or fruits sale number whether they can be easy or diffcult to sell in New Zealand supermarkets , if these farming workers can own encough farming knowledge or skill to know how to pick up fruits method and make judgement to know whether it is right time to pick up the kind of fruits from the trees , as well as know how feed this pigs, sheeps, cows to eat food in order to let they are better health. Consequently, their farming behaviors which can let these animals can provide the best taste and enough meat from these animals to let New Zealander to buy to eat from New Zealand any one supermarket. Even these New Zealand farming workers can know whether the kinds of fruits, e.g. oranges, apples, gapes etc. fruits whether they ought be picked up from the trees at the right time. Consequently, they can make judgement to decide to pick up any kinds of the best taste fruits to let any one New Zealander to buy to eat from any one supermarket in New Zealand. Otherwise, if they do not make judegement to know whether the kind of fruit ought not be picked up because they still need longer time to continue grow up to increase fruit size and better taste from the trees in order to let any one fruit buyer can feel better taste when they eat this kind of fruit later. If they can buy this kind of fruit to eat later, then this New Zealand farmer's his fruit buyers can buy the best taste of this kind of fruit to eat from an yone supermarket in New Zealand. Consequently, many New Zealand supermarkets will choose to buy any kinds of fruits from this farmer fruit supplier when they feel this farmer's fruits can provide more better taste fruits to compare other farmers' fruits.

Thus, due to New Zealand is one farming main income source country. It's any kinds of fruits and meats need to be export to overseas to sell , instead of local sale. It's GDP percent is very high to whole country 's overall income source. So, any one New Zealand farmer individual and any one farming worker individual working behavior will influence its economy whether it is influenced to grow or recession possible. Moreover, it also seems that farming workers' farming knowledge and skill will influence themselves farming daily activities to achieve the aim of the number of increase or decrease to any kinds of fruits whether they are better taste or the number of increase of decrease to any kinds of meats whether they are better taste to supply to any one New Zealand fruit or meat buyers to eat from any one New Zealand supermarket. So, it implies that any one New Zealand farming worker individual farming behavior may influence any kinds of fruits or any kinds of meat taste because they are transported to any one supermarket to sell in New Zealand.

Consequently, if New Zealans had many farmers can teach god farming knowledge and skill to let their any one farming workers know how to decide judgement to decide when it is right time to pick up any kinds of fruits from trees , or how to grow them on soil in order to let they can grow rapidly. Then, many different kinds of fruits can be provided to let any one New Zealanders can eat the best taste of fruits when their fruits are supplied to any one New Zealand supermarkets. Even, if they knew how to feed foods to pigs, cows, sheeps to eat daily. Then they can be more health and they can provide the best taste of meats to let any one New Zealanders can buy their meats from any one New Zealand supermarkets. Moreover, their fruits and meats can be transported to overseas to let any one country fruits or meats buyers can choose any kinds of New Zealand meats and fruits to buy to eat from themselves countries supermarkets. Then, many overseas fruit and meat buyers will perfer to choose New Zealand any kinds of fruits or meats to buy to compare other countries fruits or meats to buy when they go to any one local supermarkets.

On conclusion, it seems that New Zealand farming workers themselves farming behavior may influence their farming employers any kinds of fruits or meats sale number and income because their farming task behaviors must influence whether their fruits or meats taste are the better taste or worse taste to compare their other local farmers (the farmer competitors) whose fruits or meats taste. If tthe farmer's any one farming worker can be trained to learn how to know to feed animals skill and when is the most right time to pick up any kinds of fruits from trees or how to grow them on the soil methods. Due to these farming worker individual farming behavior may influence his different finds of fruits and meats sale number to be increase or decrease, so these any one New Zealand farmer must need to depend on any one farming worker whose farming working methods, if their farming working behaviors can be the best to influence any kinds of fruits to grow rapid or any kinds of pigs, cows, sheeps animals grow up rapidly , then their sale number may be increase significantly and their taste can be improved to let any New Zealand or overseas meat or fruit buyer to buy to eat to feel from any one New Zealand or overseas supermarkets, then New Zealand's agriculture industry must be influenced to increase. In the world, any one fruit or meat buyer must choose to buy New Zealand's fruit and meat to eat in prefer to compare other countries' fruits and meats. So, New Zealand's GDP may be influenced to raise from any one New Zealand farming worker individual farming working behaviors.

Reasons why human behavior may influence economic recession or growth?

Can ourselves daily behaviors or activies influence ourselves countries' economic growth or recession? I shall attempt to explain the reasons why they have direct or indirect relationship between human behavior and economy growth or recession as below:

I shall indicate environment pollition case to attempt to explain above question. Our societies had been experiencing servious environment pollution challenge. However, environment pollution , such as air pollution is caused by air planes and vehicles emission by air planes and vehicles emission as well as water pollution is caused by plastic rubblish, or dirty water or oil or gas chemical material, these both kinds of pollution ought may bring economic recession and this both kinds of pollution are caused by human ourselves daily foolish activities.

I believe human behavior and economy and pollution which have cause and effect relationship. I shall analyze this environment pollution case to explain why they have case and effect relationship between human foolish behavior and environment pollution and economic recession as below:

When global societies had many people like to buy cars to drive to bring emission to fresh air on the roads as well as many manufacturing factories will bring emission to pollute fresh air in their manufacturing processes. Factories and cars will bring air pollution , due to factories need to pollute fresh air in order to manufacture many products and car owners need to drive their cars to go to offices or leisure places. Their cars will also bring emisson to pollute fresh air. On consequence, car owners themselves frequent driving behaviors and factory workers themselves frequent manufacturing behaviors may bring environment pollution. Technology or human behavior whether may influence economic growth or recession. Moreover, air planes also brings emission to pollute air when they are flying in sky. Also, when ships bring oil pollution or sea plastic rubblishs bring pollution to global oceans.

In fact, manufactuers and cars owners, such as factories workers manufacturing behaviours ans car owners driving behaviors and pilots driving air planes flying behaviors and ships transport behaviors, which may cause plastic rubblish, oil or gas emission to sky or sea or on the road to cause ocean and air pollution is serious. However, human ourselves need to buy cars to drive to satisfy ourselves driving leisure or enjoyment, travelers need to catch air planes to travel to enjoy leisure needs, factories workers need help factories to manufacture many products to sell to customers to satisfy their using needs. oil exploration needs to find lands to explore new oil lands.

All of these business and leisure activites may bring serious air and water pollution. However, due to serious air and water pollution will bring earth warming challenge , such as some countries temperature will be influences to rise up to 40 degree or higher br earth warming. However, earth warming is caused by air and ocean pollution. Pollution must be caused by human ourselves, driving cars leisure and factories manufacturing business activities. Hence, if human decided to continue to do these foolish behaviors, we only pursue to manufacture different kinds of industrial products or drive cars to enjoy leisure aims, but we also neglect ourselves behaviors may bring environment pollution. Then, earth warming or earth temperature will be influenced to rise up absolutely in long term. Moreover, if our future earth will be influenced to bring serious high temperature effect by human ourselves these foolish behaviors.

On consequencey, warth warming will bring serious economic losses in possible because when ourselves earth temperature had been influenced to rise up to 40 degree or high. Ourselves health will be caused poor, due to we will feel difficult breath, we must need often tried and hard to work, due to our nervous and health will be influenced to poor by pollution and earth warming effect. Also, we need to pay more money to see doctors when we had long life. Then, our societies will lose may strong labors to help manufacturers to work, e.g. factories will reduce workers number to help manufacturers to produce more different kinds of products, due to workers health is general poor. Due to lacking enough workers to manufacture products, our societies will begin to reduce enough supply number of products to sell to global consumers to satisfy their use needs.

On conclusion, in behaviroal economic view, our societies will lose many labors due to their bodies are not health by air and water pollution. Global economic and business activities will be influenced to worse by global workers reducing number reason. So, economic recession will begin to occur in possible when pollution reaches the serious level.

CHAPTER FOUR

Technology or human behavior whether may influence economic growth or recession

Labors behavior or robot improves organizational performance

Organizations are increasingly using innovative technology solutions to implement performance management best practices and automate tedious manual processes. Cloud-based performance management systems are making advanced capabilities and technologies like machine learning, predictive analytics, and chatbot coaching affordable to companies of all sizes. These systems also offer quick implementation schedules, no IT support requirements, and automatic upgrades.

When selecting an automated performance management solution, make sure to do your research. Some solutions offer nothing more than an electronic appraisal form, while others offer complete best-of-breed performance and goal management. The best solutions include:

It is especially important that technology provides us with access to performance data and the ability to evaluate progress against goals, compare average manager ratings, easily access performance levels of individuals and use this data to support decision making. Aggregating and analyzing data in traditional paper-based forms is often too time-consuming and costly.

The road to effective performance management isn't always an easy one, but making manageable changes, step-by-step, will bring about significant results. The points below act as a reminder of some of the key elements of a successful process.

Raising employee individual satisfactory method

What is Employee Satisfaction? Employee satisfaction or job satisfaction is, quite simply, how content or satisfied employees are with their jobs. Employee satisfaction is typically measured using an employee satisfaction survey. Factors that influence employee satisfaction addressed in these surveys might include compensation, workload, perceptions of management, flexibility, teamwork, resources, etc.

These things are all important to companies who want to keep their employees happy and reduce turnover, but employee satisfaction is only a part of the overall solution. In fact, for some organizations, satisfied employees are people the organization might be better off without. Satisfaction doesn't mean high performance or engagement. HR ideas and strategies focused on how to improve employee satisfaction oftentimes have results that demoralize high performers.

Employee satisfaction and employee engagement are similar concepts on the surface, and many people use these terms interchangeably. The importance of knowing the difference between satisfaction and engagement is critical for an organization to make strategic decisions to create a culture of engagement. Employee satisfaction covers the basic concerns and needs of employees. It is a good starting point, but it usually stops short of what really matters. Employee satisfaction is the extent to which employees are happy or content with their jobs and work environment.

Compare that with this definition of employee engagement.

Employee engagement is the extent to which employees feel passionate about their jobs, are committed to the organization, and put discretionary effort into their work. By contrast, Passion, commitment, and most importantly, discretionary effort... Engaged employees are motivated to do more than the bare minimum needed in order to keep their jobs. They have a strong sense of purpose and leadership. They love to be challenged. Engaged employees are the engine of a company, and their performance is proof of this. The importance of engagement cannot be overstated. Satisfied employees are merely happy or content with their jobs and the status quo. For some, this might involve doing as little work as possible. An employee satisfaction survey will not diagnose key factors that can help an organization improve engagement and performance.

Turnover vs. Unwanted Turnover

Some level of turnover is healthy for all companies. Employees who are not adding value or who are not a good fit for the company leave, making way for fresh new perspectives and new energy. We could call this healthy turnover. By contrast, unwanted turnover happens when a company loses talented employees that they want to keep.

Talented and motivated employees expect more from companies. For these employees, job satisfaction includes a different set of criteria. They want to be engaged and empowered. They want to be challenged and pushed. They want their work to have meaning. They want a sense of purpose. A culture of continuous improvement and the importance of professional development opportunities for employees to grow and advance their careers, to better their performance, are key factors that contribute to the engagement of high performers.

Why is employee satisfaction a potential problem?

The problem with employee satisfaction is that it does not focus on the things that are important to your most talented staff. A happy or content employee might be quite satisfied with a job that requires very little effort. This employee might be perfectly content doing the bare minimum required to keep his or her job. These employees are likely "very satisfied" with their jobs. They usually lack leadership and purpose. Their performance might be "good enough". They are unlikely to leave the company, but they are not necessarily adding value.

As opposed to satisfied employees, engaged employees add value by pushing limits, driving growth and innovation. Organizations that embrace a value-centric, engagement focus, too, have to push limits, Companies with an engagement strategy provide informal and formal learning experiences in order to create significant opportunities for employees so employees feel valued and recognized for their work. Engaged employees will often snatch up these opportunities, satisfied employees often will not.

Employee satisfaction surveys can lead an organization down the wrong path. As a company, if you focus on increasing the wrong kind of employee satisfaction, you risk entrenching those employees who are adding the least value while driving your most talented employees out. By employing an engagement survey, asking the right questions, measuring the right factors with benchmarked results, questions and results backed by statistics, your organization can construct a strategic plan to improve employee engagement and, in turn, performance.

The importance of management skills is essential, if any organizations hope to raise efficiency or improve performance. Organizations need to learn how to balance hard and soft skill, how to manage social and human skills whch reflect the ability to get along with other people are increasingly important attributes at all levels of management.

Managers ought need to spend most time operating between the " hard skills" , such as conducting disciplinary matters or how to allocate of budgets, and " soft skills" , such as counselling, or giving support and advice to a member of staff. Managers also needed to be trained to raise technical competence, related to specific tasks, how to supervise and train subordinate staffs, and with day-to-day subordinate staff, and with day-to-day operations concerned in the actual production of goods and services; social and human skills relates to interpesonal relationship in working with and through other people, and how to judge to achieve effective teamwork and direction, and leadership of staff to achieve co-ordinated effort to particular situation and flexibilty in adopting the most appropriate style of management, raising conceptual ability in order to view he complexities of the operations of the organization as a whole, including environmental influences.

Mc Donald soft skill organizational behavior

It also involves decision-making skills, relates to the overall making of the organization and to its stragegic planning in long time, such as McDonald restaurant has good strategic management to manage its global branches of franchise restaurants in organizational behavioral view successfully. So, it can attract many investors buy its franchises to learn how to do McDonald fast food restsurants . It's investors number is increasing, due to it has good significant organizational behavior as well as its managers know how to apply " soft skills" and " hard skills" to manage them effectively.

So, organizational behavior and organizational performance seems have close relationship. If the organization can build the most effective and efficient organizational behavior, managers know how to manage employee individual behavior, then the performance ought will be improved , even customers won't complaint or feel unsatisfactory easily, they will feel satisfactory to their staffs service performance, such as McDonald fast food restaurant case, global McDonald fast food franchise restaurants eating customers complain bumber is low in general, because instead of their front line service staffs performance and attitude can let them to feel satisfactory, The most influential soft skill to bring its fast food eating customers feel satisfactory or they are persuaded to choose its sale service to replace other similar fast food restaurants sale service. The reason is because that , when they buy its fast food, or soft drink, they must be arranged to give one number ticket. So, they do not need to spend long time to queue in any McDonald fast food restaurants, they can leave McDonald restaurant to go to other places and they wont' worry that McDonald staffs forget to make their fast food or soft drink when they leave. Because they can give the number ticket to indicate their number to the staff to take their fast food or soft drink any time. For example, if the eating customer's ticket number is 30, and the screen indicates next number future cooking is 10, then he will feel that he can leave McDonald to spend about 15 minutes to come back. Even, if his coming back time is exceed 15 minutes, and the screen indicates number is 40. Although, he is late, but he may ask the staff to take his fast food or soft drink immediately. So, he does not need to worry about that he can take his fast food or soft drink even he is late to come back. So they avoid to queue long time in McDonald, they can come back after half hour, even after one hour. When they come back, they only need to give their number ticket to confirm that the had paid money to buy fast food or soft drink. When the front line staff see that number from their ticket. They will go to kitchen to take their prepared fast food or soft drink to give them immediately. it is one effective time management " soft skill" to avoid eating customers feel angry or bad emotion when they need to queue in long time in any one Mc Donald restaurant. They can choose to leave Mcdonald restaurants any long time. It is one efficient and effective 2 soft skill customer service management skill in any one nowadays McDonald front line . So , it's success depends on its front line staff " don't need eating people to queue long time" in any one McDonald restaurant.

Convenient framework of analysis of organizational behavior

Any organizations ought need have a convenient framework of analysis if they hope to manage their organizational behavior efficiently. I shall explain what a convenient framework of organizational behavior analysis means as below:

The top level is what nature and purpose of the organization, then next middle level concerns learning how to manage " behavior of people", " process of management", " organizational context" , next is middle level learning how to adapt any environment influences. The final process to any organizations. They hope to achieve improving organizational performance in success as well as organizational processes as well as how to execution of work to the most success.

It is one important service soft skill method to let global McDonald restaurants can continue to attract many eating people to choose to but their fast food or soft drink , instead of reduced price or coupon sale method in global fast food restaurant market. So, its success depends on how to mix of the practical and the soft skill service performance strategy to eating customer long time queue bad emotion theoretical psychological strategy, it must be linked to a single aim, such as Mc Donald has its single aim to front line staffs, is that how to avoid eating people need to stay in McDonald restaurant to queue long time to let them to feel angry and unsatisfactory to its global any McDonald franchise restaurants. So it comfirms that , many its global eating people don't like to queue and to stay in McDonald long time, when the Ms Donald has many people are staying in McDonald in busy time. Thus, in organizational behavioral view, they will be persuaded to choose to buy MsDonald fast food in perference, because its unique service feature, when other fast food restaurants can not implement this front lines do not need queue method in their fast food restaurants. It implies that effective front line service skill may be one important factor to influence any clients' choices in preference.

How to apply hard skill and soft skill to solve inefficient problem?
The theme of inefficiency will experience to any organizations, if they lack effective organizational behavioral management strategy. It assumed that workers who were not good at one particualr task, would be best at some other tasks in any teams. There is however, no certainty of this in practice. It concerns workers from an engineering view point and as machines , but the one best way of performing a task is not always the best method for every worker. So, the reduction of physical movement to find the one best way is or always beneficial and some " wasteful" movements are essential to the overall rhythm of work.

So, if the organization hopes to achieve effective organizational behavior, the organization needs to concern these soft skill and hard skill issues they may include:

1. High wages from increased output.

2. The removal of physical strain from doing works the wrong way.

3. Development of the workers and the opportunity for them to undertake tasks , they were capable of doing and

4. Elimination of the " boss" and the duty of management to help workers.

For example on factory raising efficient organizational behavior aspect, the factory may implement these soft skill and hard skill both strategies, such as: To assist the stores in better customer service by having the merchandise ready to go on the floor, saving space in the stockroom, and creating customer goodwill, to increase the units per hour produced, to performance the job duties as efficiency and effectively as possible, avoiding bureaucracies organization, it emphasised the importance of administration based on experise (rules of experts) and administration based on discipline (rules of officials). Because one when burea staffs are working in one serious or strict bureaucracies organization, they will feel not happy and unsatisfactory to their manager behavior. So, managers' soft management skill ought often need to revise when need to be changed to be better or improve their performance, such as:

The tasks of the organization are allocated as official duties among the various positions, there is an implied clear -out division of labor and a high level of specialisation, a hierarchical authority applies to the organization of offices and positions, uniformity of decisions and actions is achieved through formally established systems, of rules and regulations. Together work a structure of authority , this enables the coordination of various activities within the organization, an imperaonal orietnation is expected from officials in their dealings with clients and other officials. This is designed to result in rational judgments by officials in the performance of their duties as well as employment by the organization is based on technical qualifications and constitues a lifelong career for the officials, e.g. how to apply specialisation more to the job than to the person undertaking the job. This makes for continuity because the job usually continues of the present job holder leaves, hierarchy of authority it makes for a sharp distination between administrators and the administered or between management and workers, within the management ranks these are clearly defined levels of authority, system of rules aims to provide for an officials and impersonal operaton, sules are generally stable although some rules may be changed as modified with impersonality means that how allocation and exercise authority should not be complex.

Robotic how helps labours to avoid adnormal working hours

Robotic had direct relationship to influence division of labor in order to avoid labours need work long time in themselves organizations. When the organization applies robotics to assist labours to work togather. It will bring improving efficiency and productive increasing effort advantanges, when their efficiency is improved. Then many labours won't need to work long time, such as adnormal working hours. So, robotic participation is a kind new change by introducing new norms to identify performance inadequately participation, where task forces as set up to develop implementation and identify stakeholders persuasion. when implementation robotic technology and human working together stategies are delegated to technical staff or experts who then sell their ideas back to decision markers and finally, where decision-makers who control and personal power when avoiding any form of only indvidual manual labours participation to any task.

Hence, when the organization can apply robotics to participate to any tasks. Then, its efficiency will raise and productivity will also improve. Consequently, the abnormal working hours challenges will reduce, workers can be happy to work.

● Why can robotic participation assist workers do not need to work overtime or need to work adnormal hours often?

I assume that when one organization , e.g. factory will need to increase its productive number in order to achieve sale negotiation with its suppliers , but it has no enough workers to do this sudden increasing productive number task in this time. If it can have robotic to participate its productive task, then its workers will have more chance to avoid overtime hours work. Them worker individual working emotion will be better or enjoy to do their work or more working satisfactory or positive working attitude or improving performance for themselves organization's benefits. They won't feel difficult to produce these sudden increasing products immediately in this time. So, robotic can help workers to solve increasing productive number challenge.

However, robotic;s productive efficiency can be measured and assessment difficulties with technology produce systemic difficulties in managing organizations , (AI, intelligent intelligence or robotic manufacturing technology) and organization's duel natures as increasing productive and process suggest that sociotechnical frameworkers need to change significantly to accommodate longitudinal vires of technology, as well as (AI) or robotic manufacturing technology has increasing become. The manufacturing price is by which tooks and factory workers in the organization change in response to increasing productive demands in this sudden product manfacture number increasing situation.

● Robotic participation will bring these benefits

The " abnormal working hours need" organization will earn advantages from robotic's working participation. When robotics become manager's increasing productive aim of increasing in any projects that in present value terms cost less than the benefits, they bring in , i.e. increasing in positive net present value terms cost less than the benefits, they bring in, i.e. investing in positive value of factory electricity expenditure, reduces overtime working hours increasing wage cost .

So, robotic participation will help the factory reduces long time electricity expenditure cost, the overtime productive hours wage extra cost, when workers do not need to spend long abnormal working hours in factory. Their wage cost and factory electricity cost must reduce. Moreover, productive number will also increase, when the factory can let many robotics' participation to attribute to work for any factory productive prodject tasks with labours together in the factory.

The real asset to the factory may also include: robotic tangibel, instead of machinery to the factory, factories and offices, when robotic's role is productive workers or robotic may be intangible, suchas robotic technical expertise, even the reducing abnormal working hours will be intangible asset because the factory won't often need labours work overtime, then wage cost increases. So, robotic's task participation can increase the factory's real tangible asset benefit as well as intangible technical expertise benefit both, as well as reducing electricity expense, when the robotic can help the factory to manufacture many products, efficiency raises, machine electricity expense will also decreases as well as without none abnormal or overtime working hours need to any workers, then abnormal overtime wage will need to pay , due to robotic productive took assistance to every labour in the factory.

Robotic's productive participation can also help the factory to increase efficient use of assets. I assume the facrory manager owns a relatively small working worker teams that employs them to work to finish the productive project task. In general, the small working worker teams need to spend one hour to manufacture every product in themselves four productive steps. However, if robotic's participation to assist their four teams. Then, they only need half to finish to manufacture every product. So, average their every product productive time can be shortened half hour . Although, the factory may need to spend one time payment expenditure to buy the robotic, buy in long time, the robotic can help them to manufacture double number of product from one piece to two piece product every hour. It is efficient use of robotic asset to help the factory to raise productive number, when the factory does not to spend extra wage to employ extra employees to help it to raise product double productive number from one piece to two pieces product every hour. Hence, robotic's participation to manufacture process can also help the factory to achieve efficient use of assets to raise product productive number.

However, before the factory makes final decision to buy the robotics to assist workers' productive product number raises in order to achieve, these benefits, such as efficient use of resource or asset benefit, avoiding abnormal or overtime working hours need to workers, or extra overtime wage cost, even workers' poor working emotion, productive number increases, electricity expense cost reduces etc. benefits.

It needs to make evaluate properly the results of a risk analysis exercise. They may include: What is the range of possible values for the main product number outputs in the factory? What is the expected rate of return ? What is the downside of this robotic manufacturing investment? How could the factory cope with the downside? Is there any combination of uncertainties that result in robotic's manufacturing participation consequences? Which are that main uncertainty drivers cause the variation in profits or in costs? Can robotic manufacturing participation reduce these uncertainties? How does the risk return profit of this robotic manufacturing participation project companies to other alternatives, e.g. increasing workers number or increasing machines number or increasing workers and machines number both method in order to raise product productive number in long time?

However, risk analysis does not provide simple answers to this factory's manager, such as decision to buy robotics , instead of it provides a means of exploring the trade off between risk and return. It is also an interactive process. Once the factory manager has identified the main uncertainty drivers, he needs to think about ways to reduce these uncertainties by taking advantages of various " increasing product productive opportunities" , market research etc. But risk analysis is certainly a valuable tool for coping with a world in which just about everything is uncertain, such as this manufacturing robotic purchase decision case.

● How robotic reduces restaurant labours working hour

Robotic can apply to a restaurant chain to help it to avoid abnormal working hours to waiters and cookers. I assume that the restaurant has many restaurant chain in any countries. Because it is one famous restaurant and its food taste is good. So, it can attract many eating clients choose to go to its different restaurants to eat in different countries. Hence, every day, its eating clients number is increasing rapidly. Every day , restaurant chain eating clients number is increasing from average 100 to 200 per day. Although, it has many eating clients, but it's waiters and cookers need to often work overtime or work abnormal hours from 8 hours to 12 hours per day, even more hours. Moreover, these challenge will occur to its every restaurant chain in any countries. They may include: level of long waiting time to customers per restaurant. If it hopes to keep its service quality. It can not often need its waiters and cookers work overtime or abnormal work hours. If cookers need often to cook meals in kitchen more than 8 hours. Their meal perceived quality will be worse, when they feel tried to cook. Then, when eating clients feel their meals' perceived quality is worse. Then, they won't like to pay the same price to pay its meals spending on worse quality. Hence, the restaurant chain's revenue will be influenced to fall down. When, its cookers can not keep to cook the same good taste meals to every eating clients to eat every day. Even, their number of restaurant will be influenced to reduce, due to waiters need to spend abnormal working hours to serve eating clients as well as cookers need to spend abnormal working hours to serve eating clients. When clients feel other restaurants can replace any one of this chain restaurants. Then, number of restaurants will be influenced to reduce.

If this restaurant can apply robotic to help cookers to cook simple meals, e.g. vegetable, beef , pock etc. food . They can share their cooking load. Then, these cookers won't feel tried to cook when its eating clients number is increasing. Also, they may not need to work overtime, due to robotic may replace any one cooker to cook simple or complex meals. So, they can still work 8 hours, and meal quality can keep the best perceived to any one eating client when they eat in any one restaurant chain in any one country. Also, when this restaurant chain can apply robotic waiters to help them to deliver any meals to any one eating client's table immediately from kitchen, even robotic can give menu information choice to let any one eating client to make the meal eating decision rapidly, when they need to enquire any one waiter, but there is none any one waiter can serve them immediately. Then, serving robotic can help any one waiter to reduce work pressure and let every eating client feels satisfactory service , when robotic can serve to solve their meal menu choice enquire need.

The most important successful factor is that waiters do not need work overtime to serve many eating clients , when any one restaurant chain needs to increase opening hours to 12 hour or more per day. Serving robotic can help them to do eating client meal menu enquiring choice introducing service task any time , even after 8 hours normal working hours. They can replace any one waiter to do the same restaurant service task after 8 hours. So, waiters do not need spend overtime to work every day. They won't feel tried also, due to any one robotic's service can help than to serve their clients. Hence, it implies that future robotic can help any workers to avoid overtime to do work or need to work abnormal hours in possible.

How robotic changes global future labour market

● Applying management science equation to develop artificial intelligence to do management strategy

How to apply management science equation to develop artificial intelligence to help organizations to solve problem, I shall indicate the management science process may be applied to artificial intelligence mind technology as below:

Any management science techniques may include these steps: First step: From observation, then second step: Defining problem, then third step: model construction, then fourth step: solution finding, then fifth step: implementation management strategy.

From solution stage to implementation stage. Any organization must need to find information in order to achieve the most effective implementation method. Finally, from implementation stage, the organization may give feedback to problem definition step. Model construction step and solution step in order to revise whether this implementation method can be achieved the best aim to satisfy the organization's mission need.

A management scientist is a person skilled in the application of management science techniques. On the observation step, the system must be continuously and closely observed. So that the problems can be identified as soon as they occur or are anticipated. Then, on the definition of the problem stage, the problem must be clearly and defined. Then, on the model construction stage, a management science model is an abstrate representation of an existing problem situation. It can be the form of a graph or chart , e.g. a business from that sells a product. The product costs $5 to produce and sells for $20. The model that computes that total profit that will accurate from the items sold is z= $20-5x .

In this equation x represent the number of units of the product there are sold, and I represents the total profit that results from the sale of the product. The symbols x and z are variable . The term variable is used because no set number value has been specified for these items. The number of units sold, x and profit, z can be any amount (within limits).

They can vary, these two variables can be further distinguished. z is a dependent variable, because its value is dependent on the number of units sold, x is independent variable, because the number of units sold is not dependence on anything else , in this equation.

On the model solution stage, once models have been constructed in management science, they are solved using the management science techniques presented in this text. A management science solution technique usualy applies to a specific type of model. Thus, the model type and solution methods are both part of the management science techniques. We are able to say that a model is solved, because the model represents a problem.

On implementation stage, the final step , the management science process for problem solving is how to implementation the stage. Implementation is the actual use of the model once it has been developed or the solution to the problem. The model was developed to solve. This is a critical , but often overlooked step in the process. It is not always a given that once a model is developed or a solution found is automatically used. Frequently, the person responsible for putting the model or solution to use is not the same person who developed the model and thus, the user may not fully understand how the model works or exactly what it is supposed to do. individuals are also sometimes hesitant to change the normal way, they do things or try new things.

In this situation, the model and solution may get pushed to the side or ignored although if they are not carefully explained and their benefit fully demonstrated. If the management science model and solution are not implemented, then the effort and resources used on its developed have been wasted. Hence, the management science equation models may be applied to artificial intelligent technological tool to learn to help future organizations to solve management challenges, these models may include as below:

Break even analysis, graphical solution, sensitivity analysis, linear math programming analysis, linear math programming technique, probabilistic technique, network technique, forecasting, analytical process, linear programming, multiciteria decision making, nonlinear programming, mathematical equation and function inventory and operational management.

Thus, if artificial intelligence can learn above these management science equation model, then it can help any organizations to solve any management strategic challenges.

● How to apply management skills to let artificial intelligent robotic to learn

The management skills, they can be let robotic to learn. They may include: Management skill is general theory of management . It may include these principles. Division of work, specialization, authority, formal positional authority, discipline, unity of command, unity of direction, subordination of individual interests, remuneration, centralization scalar chain (line of authority), order, equity, stability of personnel, initiative.

Management process period means focuses on the management. Functions of planning, controlling, organizing, staffing and learning. Management theory jungle means to the division of thought that resulted from the multiple approaches to studying the management process. Systems approach to management means that a way of thinking about the job of managing that provides a framework for visualizing internal and external environmental factors as a whole.

Contingency approach to management theory means that different situations and conditions require different management approaches. The Japanese management movement and theory z means their emphasis an individual responsibility with the collected decision making, slow evaluation and promotion for employees.

Robotics can learn communication skill to help organization to let managers and staffs to communicate more easy in order to achieve improving working efficiency and performance in different . So, robotic is a good message sender, he can help managers to deliver any urgent or confident message to let different department staffs to know immediately. Communication is as a management skill reasons may include: Managers must give direction to the people who work for them. Managers must be able to motivate people, managers must be able to convince customers that they should do business with them. Managers must be able to absorb the ideas of others. Managers must be able to persuade other people. An interpersonal communication is an interactive process between individuals that involves sending and receiving verbal and nonverbal messages.

The interpersonal communication process: from sender (event or condition generates information). This creates a message. The sender , such as message communication sender , robotic is such as a manager assistant, needs to initial message communicated both verbally and nonverbally. To the receiver (perceives the message, dervies meaning and reacts to the message). Then, the receiver needs to reply message communicated both verbally and nonverbally , sometimes referred to as feedback to the sender, perceives messages dervies meaning and reacts to the message from robotic message assistance between any organizational departments.

Hence, if the manager can let robotic remember any important and urgent messages to help him to send any verbal or nonverbal message to communicate between individuals, especially between the manager and subordinates , it is critical to achieving organizational objectives, and as a result, to managing people effectively. Estimates vary,but it is generally agreed that since managers spend must of their time with their dubordinates, effective communication is criticial to the wise and effective use of then time.

● Why does robotic need to learn customer satisfaction skill

Developing good listening skills to robotic is also important in management skill. Active listening means absorbing what another is saying and responding to the person's concerns. Listening , know how to listen is an important part of dealing with customers . Using active listening skills can help robotics understand why customers are dissatisfied. Responding : The way robotics, respond to complaints can be just as important as the way, they solve the customer's problem. Businesspeople should always be courteous and friendly when dealing with customers. Managers need to determine what went wrong and figuring out what they can do to solve the problem as well as making sure the customers are satisfied.

Hence, teaching robotics can learn how to determine to know whether customers have satisfied their services or their needs and giving feedback they receive from the customers. Written and overall communication is the most communication method for any robotic needs to learn communication skills. Writing communication may include: email, letters, draft report, memo, oral communication is formal and takes place at meetings or interviews or phone.These communication skills are robotics need to learn in any organization.

Moreover, robotic also needs to learn rational skills how to make the most reasonable decision making. The learning steps may include: recognize the need for a decision, establish, rank and weigh the decision criteria, gather, available information and data, identify possible alternatives, evaluate each alternative with respect to all criteria and select the best alternative.

Moreover, robotic also needs to learn satisficing skill. What is satisficing approach? The satisficing approach is a believing the assumptions of generally unrealistic. The capacity of the human mind for formulating and solving complex problems is very small compared with the size of the problems whose solution is required for objectively rational behavior , or even for a reasonable approximation to such objective rationality.

The steps of satisfied skill that robotic needs to learn. The first step: satisfied with best alternative found ? " yes", then making decision, if " no" search for additional alternative, then value of new alternative found either achieving value of best previous alternative or achieving current level of aspiration.

So, satisficing approach assumes: If person's knowledge of alternatives and criteria is limited. People act on the basis of a simplified, ill-structured, mental abstraction of the real world. People do not attempt to optimize , but will take the first alternative that satisfied their current level of aspiration , it is called satisficing.

An individual's level of aspiration concerning a decision fluctuates upward and download, depending on the values of the most recently identified alternatives. If the decision marker, such as robotic's knowledge of alternatives is incomplete, the individual commit optimize , but can only satisfice. Optimizing means selecting the best possible alternative, satisficing means selecting the first alternative, that meets the decision maker's such as robotic's minimum standard of satisfaction .

Assumption , it is based on the belief that the criteria for a satisfactory alternative are determined by the person's current level of aspiration. Level of aspiration refers to the level of performance a person expects to attain, and it is impacted by the person's prior successes and failures.

These environment factors will influence any robotic decision maker's decision . They may include: the patterns of the organizational manager his authority by the formal organization structure, for example, when robotic is one management strategic tool in a military organization , it requires to learn a different style of decison making than a volunteer organization does, whether the organization's formal and informal group structures. The decision maker, such as robotic's superiors and subordinates, personalities, backgrounds and expectations of these people influence the decision markers. So, robotic's decision making may be revised by his mangers , the labor market, the political climate and competition. These factors will influence the robotic's final decision making can be accepted or not by the organization.

● Worker lazy behavior applies to robotic

Why can robotic help workers to avoid lazy. Taylor's studies find that enterprisers can not satisfactorily benefit from workers and believed that forming and programming of doing works should be regulated by a scientific analysis and more output would be gained if they were standardized . He found about human factor may include: Lazy and least work, unproductive can be avoided when robotic can assist workers together in any organizations.

Robotic also is observed that this unproductive work order and environment existing in enterprise may give big damages at a degree tat can reach to losses at an extent effecting national economy. Some radical decisions must be taken from robotic to turn factors causing inefficiency ad effecting production negatively into neutural or to minimize them. Robotic can assist worker to avoid lazy working behavioral worker management principle may include: workers and managers must work according to scientific principles rather than working haphazardly , when carrying out organizational activities, organizational activities must be performed in a coordinated and consistent way, not in an inconsistent way, organizations and their methods, rather than submitting low unpredictiveness , must reject this and must try to provide the highest productivity, each labor must be parted to sub-factors forming it, when defining activities which workers and robotic must carry out, not only intuition and experience, but also scientific methods must be chosen, that say, the most suitable staff member and robotic must be chosen to work together in order to achieve raising efficiency and improve performance aims.

Why can robotic's participation assist workers to improve performance? Because people whose mental and physical skills are sufficient for works being standardized must be chosen, that say, the most suitable staff member must be chosen, specialization in every part of a defined labor and robotic must be provided. When robotic and workers work together, standards and specialization of workers, functions, such as organization, planning, controlling and coordination in management.

On the contrary to the representatives of scientific management's aiming to increase productivity of by dealing with the form of works' and robotic's being done and work design more at factory level. So, robotic and workers work together, they can raise productivity, economical efficiency and rationalism. Views as them both about the human and machine cooperative factor in enterprises from the workers and robotics, instead of the ability to manage, have desired to be managed and generally avoid taking responsibility.

What is robotic participation to working environment advantages ? In every step of hierarchy, authority and duties are determined formally by pre-determined law, method and administrative regulations, labor's being distingushed to parts is carried out in according with determined rules and standards by specialized staff member, processes and communication are done in written form, workers obey to directives, as they are based an legal authority. So, robotic participation can bring benefits to staff to know how to follow company's regulation to do their task together in order to achieve the reasonable performance. It means inefficiency or low production will be reduced when robotic and workers can work together.

● How robotic and workers coordination in factory condition

The scientific management conditions in factories were unplanned, there was absence of standardization of methods of work, these was no rational method of assigning workers to their jobs and they were often placed in jobs that they preferred. The work to be done and the methods to be adopted and selection of tools were also determined by workers and robotics. When robotic and workers coordination , it can help organization to reduce a lot of waste of materials, loss or production and inefficiency, there was no coordination between departments and managers did not posses decision making skills, they had no clear idea of the responsibilities. Decisions and standards of work performance were made on the basis provision to the workers and robotics with an opportunity for a " systematic " as well as the purposed restriction of output.

Hence, the reason why robotic and workers cooperation can raise productivity or improve performance, it is based on management science on these observations, a scientific theory of management aimed at discovering the one best way of performing any task as well as increasing productivity, revolutionized the idea of optimizing productivity. So, robotic and workers cooperation focused on the most efficient way of managing and making the workers more productive.

However, robotic and workers efficient principle may include: To find the best way of doing a job, so that the best method for performing each task could be determined . The most efficient ways of completing tasks and standard work procedures were delivered to enhance productivity. It involved the scientific selection and progressive development of the workers, when robotic can participate to task with workers together. So, when robotic can participate to workers' team tasks, each worker and each robotic would be assigned responsibility for the task for which expected that management can better identify strengths and weaknesses of each worker. Robotic aims to help workers to maximize his/her capacity. The successful factors include to raise productivity, equal division of work and responsibility between managers and robotics and workers, promoting friendly cooperation between managers and workers and robotics would help management for better supervision of its workers as well as reduction of disputes between robotics and workers, raising productivity and efficiency were the primary ends of scientific management aim when robotic participation is implemented to any workers' tasks and they do not need to spend long time training, due to robotic can do the complex tasks.

In conclusion, robotic participation can bring these advantages to any organizations. They may include: reducing time and expenditure for staff training, determination of standards of performance, the real problem concerns that no one exactly knew how much work a worker was expected to do in a specific / given time, rather than following any scientific basis, e.g. time and emoton how determines the standard of work performance, avoiding functional supervision and recommended functional foremanship in the organization in which robotics can do complex tasks , when workers can do simple tasks together, managers do not need to spend long time to supervise workers , when robotics can do more complex tasks, every worker is responsible for some specific aspect of the worker's simple task, the division of work between managers and workers and robotics favoring a compute separation of the planning function from the doing function. For example, the linear system or military type of organization in which each worker is subordinate to only one boss; piecework system of wage payment means that workers did as little as possible because under prevalent system of wage hard. Avoiding piece productive number reducing problem, when robotic participation to piecework for motivate then to achieve the highest level of efficiency. Finally, robotic participation can help workers to reduce mental pressure to work, in its essence, it involves a complete mental revolution in the attitudes of workers toward their work and in the attitudes of management toward their duties and ways in which they handle their daily piece productive number problems. According to robotic participation to determining standards of work benefits, they may include that eliminating wasteful operation and piecework system of wage payment would benefit both the workers and the employer/management, which will result into a mental revolution among the workers and the management, since they would develop a cooperative attitude toward workers and managers and robotics together.

● How and why robotic participation can bring personnel selection benefit
To answer this question. we need insight in terms of human resource management . Indeed, " piece rate" , payment method is popular to be used to evaluate workers performance, but when robotic participation can help organizations to evaluate every worker wage/salary easily. For example, in factory manufacture environment, when robotic participation to workers team cooperative tasks, this wage system can motivate workers to work hard. It emphasizes the necessity of high wage and low cost per unit, and therefore the manager and workman and robotic collaboration in the selection and reducing time to train staffs when robotics can participate to every worker's tasks. It assumes that reducing training time to ever worker was taken into consideration more than systematic managerial work when robotics can participate to do complex tasks, workers can do simple tasks when they cooperate to work together.

However, robotic participation can help workers to reduce working pressure as a mental revolution rather than an means of productivity which came into fashion at that time. Thus , the cooperation with managers and workers and robotics is as an essential principle. Although, scientific method seems to adopt the increase in production, it can also solve the problems between the managers and workmen and robotics. It seems that robotic participation can help workers to raise interest to work when they only concentrate on doing the simple task part and robotic can help them to do complex task part. It assumes that every worker work performance and wage decision is based on their simple task process part to piece productive number finishing every hour, due to robotics can help them to finish the complex task process part to piece productive number finishing every hour. So, if one worker can finish 100 piece productive number simple task part every hour, but another worker can finish 200 piece productive number simple task part every hour, when robotics can participate to complex process task part to finish every product piece productive number process, it can ensure that the 200 piece productive number simple task part worker can have higher efficiency and better work performance to compare the only finishing 100 piece productive number simple task process worker. So, robotic participation can bring benefit to help organization to evaluate every worker salary level more reasonable.

● Why can robotic bring talent working place benefit and reduces long time training and development cost
The quality of a working place is determined by the quality of its employees

to a great extent. The success of many establishments depends on the labour and robotic force which has the talent to carry out the task required for the job and the ability to perform the strategic aims to the establishment. So, the success of personnel recruitment, when robotic can participate to do complex task part, So, robotic participation can help organization to choose right employee to do any simple task part, when they can finish the more piece productive number to simple task part. So, when robotic participation do not need workers to do complex task part, they only needs to concentrate on finishing the simple task part. They do not need to be trained. If the worker is one talent worker, they must not need more training time to learn how to finish the simple task part. So, robotic participation to manufacture complex task part which can help organization to know whether who is the talent worker to continue to be selected to employ , when he can finish to produce to manufacture many pieces when they only manufacture simple task part in factory. Hence, robotic participation can also help organizations to reduce long time training and development cost.

Hence, robotic participation can help organizations to measure whether whom workers can have productive efficiency or improve performance, when they only concentrate on manufacturing the simple task part to finish every product. Capitalists can not accurately know the worker's labor efficiency, when they need to manufacture every product in both simple and complex task parts. A worker is under normal working conditions and work flow can do how much work, but all too workers work less, get more salary and then by extending the worker's labor time, when robotic can not participate to assist them to manufacture complex task part. But, when robotic can not participate to their product productive process. Sone workers feel they are doing more, but they are paid less. When they need to learn to manufacture the more complex task part to every product. So, it explains that why robotic can encourage workers feel less working pressure or more lazy to finish the only simple task part to finish every product. If they only concentrate on manufacturing simple part to every product. Then , the workers who can manufacture many products when they only concentrate on manufacturing the simple task part. Their salary may be reasonable increased and they can feel more fair. Then, they won't perform poor. Also, the under manufacturing workers will be encouraged to raise productive number, if they hope that their wage can also be increased. When robotic can participate to help them to manufacture the complex task part to finish every product in the whole finishing process in the talent factory working environment. During the poor performance workers do not feel unreasonable days work often, then prevailing daily wage and general piece work wage system . It is not short coming and it can motivate their productivity to be increased in the factory talent working environment, when robotic can participate to help them to do any complex task part to every product. So, it explains why factory piece production wage system can raise productivities or efficiency when robotic can participate to help workers to do the complex task part to every product in whole manufacturing process. For example, one skilled labour wage calculation only depends on how much piece , he can produce. This skilled worker's wage rates calculation methods can not excite his piece manufacturing number in factory. The low skilled workers may apply piece wage system to excite their productivities when robotic can participate to simple task part manufacturing process. Robotic participation to complex task part, it aims to upgrade their low skills to high skilss in order to manufacture the kind of product in proficient. But for computer hardware equipment manufacturing workers example, their skills need to apply robotic scientific standardization to meet the raising efficiency and productivities needs of the production of each simple and complex task both parts. So, if the management hope the whole computer hardware manufacturing process can be improved the efficiency of the team work with the process and development of robotic technology, the proportion of brain labor is needed to increase when robotic can help the skilled workers to manufacture the complex task part of every hardware product. So, it explains why the piece wage system is suitable to skillful workers, such as computer hardware manufacturing tasks. The computer hardware organization needs to change its compensation management, pay a high wage rate in order to encourage these high skilled employees to do their work on the simple task part to computer hardware products on time. They can make corresponding incentives. Hence, robotic participation to hardware product complex task part, it can help computer manufacturing company to evaluate whether whom can be talent to learn the simple task part more easily, when they can manufacture the simple task part to finish every hardware in short time.

● How to implement the mind of strategy skills to robotic?
I shall indicate how robotic's strategic thinking process as below:
Robotics need to be learnt to own managers' judgement abilities, if organizations hope robotics can make the best strategic skills . The strategic

skills need robotic to learn , the skills may include: Deciding whether the consumers likely to favor a quality product, if " yes" robotic needs to learn hoe to reflect quality in marketing strategy . Otherwise, if " no", robotic needs to learn hoe to design analysis, or deciding whether the company can make uneconomic purchases, if " yes", learning how to improve purchase methods, replace suppliers, " no" learning how to improve production process control or deciding whether the work in pace too slow, if " yes", learning how to improve employee education and training: install incentive system, if " no", deciding there are many rework, if " no" there is too much down time. Are of these analysis strategy process which be any robotics need to learn in order to achieve the most effective strategy management skills to recommend themselves organizations how to solve any management challenges.

For this profit analysis price flexibility case to robotic to learn example, the whole learning process to make decision may include this strategic thinking to let robotic to learn: the question may be " can the ex-factory price to raised?" It has two questions possibilities:

One is " can the market price be raised? "

Then it may has two possibilities:

The first possibility is simple increase in the list price possible. Then robotic can make these solutions: price elastic, possibility of price rises differentiate by geographical areas, models or by distribution channels, results achieved by competitors (possibility of " follow-the-leader" price increase.

The another possibility is that it is possible to raise the price by changing the product model to more than cover the increased cost? Then it may make solutions: Basic consumer needs in each market segment, price elasticity, cost -benefit analysis.

The another question may be: Can distribution margins be reduced? Then, it may have three possibilities: The first possibility may be " would integration of retail outlets enable margins to be reduced?" The solutions may include: Basic economic analysis of distribution system, analysis on economic of scale, correction between number sales outlets and market coverage. The second possibility may be " could volume be maintained if only low-margain channels were used?"

Then, the solutions may include: flexibility in physical flow of goods by distribution channels, degree of motivation and sales effort exerted by different channels.

The final possibility may be " could a switch to direct sales reduce distribution margin?" Then solutions may include: analysis of long -term strategic effect, analysis of short-term,, cost-benefit and possibility of maintenance of sale skills.

All of above strategic analysis process, robotic must need to learn in order to achieve human's mind process to make the most reasonable decision making to help managers to solve challenges.

Hence robotic ought need to be trained , such as one management consultant helps the organization's manager to recommend any useful strategic in order to make the most reasonable solution. However, robotic needs to learn how to determine the critical issue. The first stage in strategic thinking is needed to know what the critical issue in the situation for its organization. Robotic needs to learn how to make strategic thinking. In problem solving, it is at the start to formulate the question in a way that will facilitate the discovery of a solution. Hence, robotic needs to learn how to find the critical question that its organization needs to solve to avoid low efficiency or poor performance causes. Discovering the most influential problem will be robotic duty.

Suppose , robotic discovers the overtime work has become serious hurt to a company to cause low profit . It needs to find solution how to reduce overtime. Recommendation may include: work harder during the regular working hours, shorten the lunch period and coffee breaks, forbid long private telephone conversation, product quality, involves the participation of all employees. So, robotic's role participation task may include: How to gather ideas, screened and later incorporated in the improvement program. Returning to this overtime problem. Suppose the question in a more solution-oriented way: Is this company's work force large enough to do all the work required? Hence, robotic's strategic thinking needs to be better than manager. Otherwise, the firm manager can attempt to solve this problem.

To this question: There can be only one of answers, " yes or no". To arrive at answer " yes", a great deal of analysis would be needed, probably including a comparison with other companies in the same industries. The historical trend of workload per employee, and the degree of automation and computerization and their economic effectiveness. On the other hand, if after careful check sales record, profit per employee, ration between direct and indirect labor, compensation with other companies, the answer should be no (i.e. the company is currently understaffed. So robotic ought to be trained to learn to make the most reasonable solution for this problem.Such as " understaffed" causes " overtime" to cause low profit reasonable recommendation to this company manager. If robotic can make this "understaffed" reason causes low profit result to let manager to solve. Then, this company manager may find this solution, the probability increases that desired adopts this robotic 's follow.

However, a shortage of suitable personnel should be sought either in staff training or in recruiting capable staff. In the other hand , if the owner is " yes" this indicates that the problem of overtime lies in the nature of the work, but in the amount of the workload. Thus, not training but adding to the work force would be the critical factor in the solution. Hence future robotic needs to how to find the critical question to cause any organization's low profit as well as making the judgement how to recommend the most reasonable solutions in order to give the most reasonable recommendation to its organization manager. All of these are future robotic needs to be learn in order to make human's strategic thinking mind.

Finally, the observed phenome to any organization's problems, in general, they may include these problems aspects that future robotics need to learn organization's strategic thinking process.

On personnel problems aspect, they may include these aspects: Increase in average age, seniority system of promotion, low mobility of personal among divisions. Then, robotic ought make the " inflexibility in organization" decision to determine of " reorganization strategy" , e.g. how to reorganization itself organization to solve its organization overall personnel problems.

On cost problems aspect, they may include these factors: Increase in number of managers, decline in morale among younger employees, increase in personnel costs, delays in new product development. If robotic can ensure those factors may cause its organization's cost problems. Then, robotic ought may make judgement because costs high with competitors to cause its cost problem.

Finally, robotic needs to learn how to plan for improving profitability determination. On strategic problem aspect, they may fall in profitability, increase in unprofitable products factors to cause strategic problems. If the organizational robotic can find these phenomena to cause strategic problems. Then , it ought make judgement to know hoe to determine to implement its revised strategic in order to solve its organization's inflexibility in corporate strategy problem.

Thus, this organization's robotic is needed to learn how to analyze its organization's current different problem aspects whether are existed to influence its organization's high cost, inflexible corporate strategy or inflexible in organization influences. Then, this robotic needs to learn how to help its manager to find the most suitable pan to reorganization or how plan for improving profitability or how revised strategies in ordr to assist its ,anger to solve present existed actual problem effectively.

In conclusion, future robotics ought need to learn strategic thinking skill in order to give the most effective recommendation to assist their managers to solve any problems if the organization hopes it can keep long time competitive effort. Thus, future management ought need robotic participation to their strategic thinking discussion in order to achieve the most excellent strategic plan implementation to win their competitors.

● How robotic can manufacturing and service job market?

In the future, when robotic participate to any organizations' tasks. It will bring significant positive and negative impact to influence global labour market change. I shall indicate as below:

when robotic participation can improve efficiency, then it will cause the low skilled workers lose job ,e.g. factory workers, restaurant waiters, cookers etc. low skilled and low educational level occupations. , if they expect employers can pay same or higher wage for these low skilled and poor performance workers in this low skilled workers group in any organizations. They will loss their jobs more easily, due to robotic may replace these low skilled and poor performance workers in any one working places.

Robotics can work in service industry, instead of factory manufacturing industry in the future, e.g. cinema front line ticket sale service staff, public bus or train or tram driver, (non manual auto AI driver), shopping center security or customer service staff etc. occupations. So , in these service market, they can not perform to satisfy customer service need, then employers will feel their services are " price out of market", due to robotic can be popular to be accepted to serve clients in any service working environment in possible. Then, these poor service performance staff's salary may be influenced to reduce, even robotic can replace them to perform better service. So, many poor performance service and manufacturing workers will lose jobs , if their service or manufacturing performance can not perform better or improve better to compare general performance level staffs.

So, robotics tasks participation may impact many poor performance workers to influence they lose their jobs , due to employers will seek better performance staffs and/or robotics can replace them. So, the unemployment ratio will have possible increase, when global employers begin apply robotics to assist workers to manufacture products or serve clients.

Robotic participation helps companies to maximize profit. The fundamental assumption of labor theory is that firms, the employers of labour seek to maximize profit. So, firms are assumed to continue ask " Can we make changes that will improve profit, when robotic is participated to either manufacturing task or service task?"

First , a firm can make changes only in variable that are within its control, because the price , a firm can change for its product and prices, it may pay for its inputs are largely determined by other (" the market"). However, robotic role can only help it to raise efficiency or improve performance. So, robotic participation can not guarantee to raise profit or profit maximization, but it can help organizaions to raise efficiency or improve performance, when robotic can assist manufacturing or service workers to work together in any manufacturing or service workplaces.

● How artificial intelligence influence e-business workers market?

E-business is popular to be applied to sell any products from website. However, when artificial intelligence is participated to e-operation management environment. It can influence some e-business labor to lose jobs , due to artificial intelligence can provide better e-service task performance to compare these e-service labor, the e-service may include, such as online customer service support or e-inventory management, e-distribution and logistics, technical infrastructure.

When any e-commerce management tasks can be applied to robotic to replace any human e-service provision workers. Then, many e-service provision workers will lose jobs. Any website e-business management tasks will apply artificial intelligent e-service provision tool to replace human e-service provision workers , when they can perform better e-service provision to manage their websites, as well as satisfy e-clients' needs.

How to operate their websites to achieve the most attracting and efficient online sale performance? For example, applying (AI) development to define the customer online purchase experience in the e-operation planning process. It may include these three steps" The first step is that developing high level customer view process, flows of the online seller's production processes. The second step is that identifying quality metics, (AI) helps the online seller to decide whether what need to be measured to indicate the quality level of the online customer's shopping experience and the quality of the production process. The final step is that identifying types of requirements. There are two types: By resource (technical, organizational and informational) as well as by operational management function. When (AI) tool can help the online organization to design e-operation planning process to improve the best online shopping experience to any one client to feel. Then, many e-service provision workers can be replaced in e-business related any e-operation management task aspect.

● How robotic becomes one kind of factor of production to the owning robotic task participation organizations?

However, robotic will be one kind of factors or production to the owning robotic task participation organizations. Instead of land, labor, capital and entrepreneurship factor of production. Robotic will be tangible talent technique manufacturing tool or service worker machine to factor of production to these owning robotic task participation organizations, as well as intangible skilled technique to upgrade works to improve individual performance or raise efficiency factor or production to these businesses.

Hence, in economics the factors of production view, robotic can be the basic inputs of any productive goods or service-producing system to businesses. When robotic participation to the shopping center, factory, restaurant, cinema , e-commerce etc. different organization tasks. It can be one kind of skilled technique worker. It has different to general labour, general labour is the mental and physical effort available to produce goods and service, the human resource. Unskilled, semi-skilled and skilled are terms that describe different types of labour. Management skill is also a type of labour.

How much a firm produces and the quality of what it produces are affected by the motivation, skills, and efforts of its labour. Japan's development from a devastated economy to an economic superpower in four decades is due in part to its highly productive human resource. However, when the organization applies robots to participate its daily task, like this one at a Joh Deere plant are capital goods that helps to mechanize and automate the production process. Hence, robotic can be one tangible machine capital to this plant, but when it can improve worker skills to be upgrade or raise efficiency, it can be also intangible skilled asset to this plant. Hence robotic may have effort to help this plant's low skilled labours to upgrade. Their low skills can be upgraded to be higher skills. Their skills can be trained to upgrade or improved from robotic's task participation in this plant. Then, this plant will have not many low skilled workers, if most of them can be upgraded skills or improve skills. It means that robotic helps this plant's low skilled workers to be trained to raise high skills when they can cooperate to work together. Then, manufacturing industry will have more high skilled workers if many plants apply robotics to participate and cooperate low skilled workers to manufacturing process. It will influence the country's factory labour market will have none high skilled workers shortage challenge, due to if many plants apply robotic participation to any workers' tasks cooperation to work together in order to improve their efficiency and raise any product productive number. Then, , due to many robotic participation , it can influence many high skilled workers number increase to the country. In consequent, the high skilled workers supply number is more than the labour demand in plant manufacturing industry. Then, the high skilled workers' salaries will be influenced to reduce. So, robotic's participation to plant manufacturing process, it may influence the high or proficient skilled workers' wages level to be gone down or reduce in the country's plant manufacturing labour market.

● Why can robotic avoid productivity challenge and the firm does not need to employ extra worker ?

Robotic's participation can help the manufacturers to avoid not enough productive number challenge and they do not need to employ extra workers . The reason is that when the plant workers can learn how to cooperate with the robotic to work together effectively. Then, their productivities ought be influenced to increase, because robotic can assist them to reduce their work pressure, when they only need to do the simple task, robotics need to help them to do complex task. In this robotic and worker long time cooperative working behavior, these factors may help them to raise productivity, they may include that: The plant do not need often to replace outdated plants and equipment, due to robotic's participation to this plant's complex task part. This plant does not need to invest in research and development to find new ways to design, produce, and market products, due to this plant had found new application for robots, this plant does not need to develop new ways to manage employees by raising their layers of management and getting workers more involved in decision making. Because robotic has assist these workers to finish complex task part in whole manufacturing process, these workers only need to concentrate on doing simple tasks part every day. For example, more robotic complex task participation firms are using self-managed teams to rejuvenate the work ethic. So, when the firm can let robotict o participate complex task part and its staffs only need to do simple tasks part as well as they do not need to spend time to participate and learn how to making decision with managers or spend time to learn in training., due to robotic's complex task part participation. So, in long time, their productivities may be influenced to raise, when they only concentrate on doing simple task part, due to robotics can help them to do complex task part daily.

However, this owning robotic complex task part participation to plants won't need to employ extra workers, but their productivities may be raised. Then, it will influence labour demand will reduce, even employers will dismiss some low skilled workers, when managers feel they can not raise productivities as well as when robotic helps them to do complex task part. It may influence the unemployed low skilled and poor performance workers number increases or/and their wage may be influenced to reduce in the country's plant manufacture industry labor market.

In conclusion, robotic's participation to complex task part, it may influence labour market to change to raise low skilled workers unemployed number, and reduces their wage level, but productivity may be influenced to increase, low skilled workers may be ungraded their skills by robotic's complex task part participation, can bring positive influence to employers, e.g. raising productivities number, increasing profit, reducing machine purchase and employee number salary expense, upgrade low skilled worker skill, or creates talent workers, reducing training time and expense. But it can bring negative influence to employeeees, e.g. it canuses low skilled worker unemployment, their wages reduce in themselves countries labor market.

How robotic brings positive and negative social change
● Why does robotic seem to McDonaldization franchise sale method
Robotic's invention can influence global society has large change. I shall explain what it seems to be similar to McDonaldization global fast food restaurant sale method in possible. How it can be franchise to commodification , ration and globalization to sell any kinds of robotic products to bring global franchise income for robotic inventors. Robot's invention can let robotic inventors to own franchise to sell their different kinds of robotic in factories, manufacturing places, factories warehouse delivering goods places, hospital room food delivery places, restaurant food

delivery places, restaurant kitchen cooking places or restaurant waiter serving clients places, shopping center securities or customer service counter places or office computer documents delivery or clerical working places etc. different kinds of service or manufacture tasks.So, robotic's influence to future service or manufacture model can be changed to machines. Many people will lose jobs if they are replaced by robotic in factories or restaurants or offices or hospitals or shopping center etc. different working environments.

If robotics inventors own franchise , it seems that it can be similar to McDonaldization global fast food restaurant to sell its robotics to different business buyers or householders to satisfy their needs. When every robotic sellers need to buy franchise from the robotic inventors. So, robotic inventors seem to be similar to McDonaldization founder to own franchise to sell its fast foods. The different view, is that robotic inventors sell robotic price must be more expensive to compare McDonaldization's fast food. So, it will influence future any business buyers or householders need to pay high price to buy any one robobit's founder's inventing robotic products when they owns franchise to sell their different robotic in society.

This phenomenon will bring social much change, such as restaurants won't need many waiters or cookers if they have robotic cookers to help them to cook food or robotic waiters help them to serve eating clients, cinemas do not need many bringing seat position serving staffs or from counter ticket sell service staffs ,because robotics can replace them to do simple servicing tasks in cinemas, factory warehouses also do not need many workers to help them to deliver goods because robotics can deliver goods to any right places very rapidly, such as Amazon is applying robotics to help their goods to deliver to any places in warehouses nowadays, they can perform more better to compare warehouse workers.Also robotic can help them to manufacture products to replace manufacture workers, so manufacturing workers number will be influenced to reduce.

● Why robotic seems to McDonaldization's operation?

They have these similar points to raising service aspects: Computerization, product-predictability, managerial control, efficiency, raising production value, quantity manufacturing value, providing excellent convenience and rapid delivery service. So, robotic franchise can be similar to McDonaldization to let robotic inventors to continue to own franchise to invent different kinds or function robotics to satisfy our different services or manufacture needs aspects.

Nowadays, education organizations had begun to attempt to apply robotics to replace teachers to teach students in classrooms, or householders had begun to apply robotics to help them to do cleaning tasks, e.g. cleaning kitchen, toilets or security job etc., even robotic can help parents to take care parent's children at home when they leave homes. So, future robotic won't only influence business jobs change aspect, it may also influence householder's life aspect. When robotic is popular to be accepted to be used for anyone. Then, the robotic inventors can be seem to McDonaldization founder have themselves own franchise to sell their unique robotics to global different countries markets. Then, our societies will feel robotics are our living part. We need to apply them to help us to do any simple . even complex tasks in order to satisfy our living needs. So, robotic's invention will be possible serious to influence our future society to become " machine man " society. Anyway, working environment, service environment or home environment will own at least one robotic to serve our organizations or homes.

Hence, robotic seems to be one kind of new resource to motivate own society to change to be more better. Our part traditional living model or living attitude is need to be change. We need to learn how to adapt the live or to work with robotic in anywhere together. Robotics seem to be our future social capital. It is rooted in social networks and social relations and is conceived as resources embedded in a high technique social structure that are accessed and/or mobilized in purposive actions. So, robotic's invention seems to one big artificial intelligent organization. The different kinds of robotic inventions will organize how to design different kinds of robotics to satisfy human's unlimited needs to be applies to different aspects in our society. For example, future public transport tool drivers, e.g. bus , tram, ferry, train, mass transit rail drivers will be replaced by robotics. Non-manual drivers will be popular to be replaced to different countries by robotic's automatic drivers. many drivers will also lose driving jobs. They will be assistant role to the robotic drivers. So, if robotic invention can be invented in success to make more accurate to drive any kinds of transport tools in order to avoid road accidents occurrence chance to be the least minimum level to compare manual drivers. Then, our societies will be non-manual driving transport tools. We need to adapt to accept or believe their driving skills must be better than manual drivers. Otherwise, we only may choose to buy cars to drive.

So, robotic will be our future important resources. They will help to do complex tasks, instead of simple tasks, e.g. seeking the suitable land or ocean to attempt to discover any new milling or oil or gas resource and help human to do the difficult exploration oil or gas tasks. We ought believe that they have much accurate judgement to compare human's talent. So, they will be talent machine to replace human to do much complex mind judgement tasks. Even, they may be space scientists to help us to find many undiscovered natural resources from outside earth or planet. When robotic can be invented to own high mind judgement effort or talent effort to compare humans. So, in science research aspect, future human scientists may be needed to accept themseleves to be robotic's assistant to assist them to do any science research tasks in laboratory, when robotic can be invented to own human talent effort.

Hence, robotic's invention will influence our societies to be changed more advanced or more fun or most technological development. Human can not predict how robotic's change to influence our future society in which aspects accurately. But, many robotic scientists are continue attempting to research robotics how to invent on which aspects to satisfy our different living needs. I believe that robotics will help us to serve our societies much better.

It is simple , that our post industrial society, and such social change is needed traditional computer will be replaced by (AI) artificial intelligence or called robotics. So, our industrial society will change to encounter technological society. It continues to fascinate those commentators seeking to understand transitions from a modern to a post-modern world also preoccupies those who prefer to think about the " transformation" society or technological society.

The invention is which global tendencies are taking hold are arguably more about countinue than they are about change. The extent to which new technologies, such as robotic invention fundamentally alter our lives is debatable. How important is the internet, for instance? Who is to say that ultimately it might prove more controlling than it is enabling? Indeed, our part most industrial society, notably as regards the spread of scientific rationality , such as robotic invention.

Our post-industrial society has none limited staying power, such as robotic's invention. The extent to which such ideas really illuminate our understanding of contemporary social life beyond the general insights provided by its technological dimension is questionable.

● Why does robotic seems to be common social commodity?

Thus robotic will be seemed to common commodity first and foremost as something to be sold and exchanged on the marketplace. It therefore had a role in determining our social position. From Marx's point of view, determined by how you actively engaged with consumer goods. When, robotic is popular to be accepted to use and robotic's manufacturing number will increase. Then, it's price will reduce,when supply is increased. The robotic's commodity therefore plays a fundamental role in relating the individual (householder user) to the capitalist system (business organization user) . It promotes a sense of false consciousness that camouflages the realities of alienation.

Robotic's commodification seems to be McDonaldization commodification, by process , by which everything is valued according to its value in the system of exchange, creates a world in which a person's (householder's or business organization's priorities become subject to the requirements of the job making or our living need.

Marx therefore believes that robotic becomes a situation in which the worker is aliented by the fact he or she no longer has ownership of the artificial commodity he or she helps to work together in any organization. The worker is a assistant who no longer is needed to do his/her tasks in his/her organization when the organization applies robotic to be own labour.

Marx (2000) therefore decides the fetishism of the commodity, such as artificial intelligence or robotic. By this, Marx means that the commodity such as robotic was a mystical quality: To the extent that objects become to the self, and are therefore ascribed a significance beyond their use-value. The robotic commodity is treated with an awe and reverence previously reserved for religion. But even, in this analysis, for Marc, the fetishism of the robotic commodity is only a by-product of independent labour to our future society.

The fetishism of the world of commodities arises from social character of the labour which produced them, such as robotic objects of utility become commodities, such as robotic only because they are products work independently of each other . The special social characteristics of employers' private labours such as robotics appear only which this exchange. Hence, Marx was certainly accurate , there can be no doubt that the process of commodification, such as robotic has reached new extremes to enter our society to bring benefit to influence our daily lives.

● How can robotic bring global social stratification positive and negative change?

Why does robotic have relationship to social stratification? Firstly, we need to know that social stratification mean? Some of the world's nations are wealthy, other poor and some in between. This division of nations as well as the layering of groups of people within a nation, is called " social stratification".

Social stratification is one of the most significant topics to discuss . It will affects one life chances, such as robotic's invention from our access to material possession to the age at which we die.

Social stratification also affects the way we think about life. If you had been born into the rich family, you can be illiterate and would assume that your children would be as well. You also would expect hunger to be a part of life and would not expect all of your children to survive. To be born into the family, however, would give you quite a different picture of the world. You would expect your children not only to survive, but to go to college as well. You can see that social stratification brings with it ideas of what we can expect out of life. So, it has different between rich countries and poor countries people, business organization AI users or householder AI users their thinking to need robotics' attitude in social stratification view.

Social stratification is a system in which groups of people are divided into layers according to their relative property, power. It is important to emphasize that social stratification does refer to individuals. It is a way of ranking large groups of people into a hierarchy according to their relative families. It is also important to note that every society stratifies its members. Some societies have greater inequality than others, bur social stratification is universal. In addition, in every society of world, gender is a basic for stratifying people. On the basic of their gender, people are either allowed or denied access to the good things offers by their society.

Hence, due to social stratification or unequal born occurs in our nowadays society, it will influence different countries people will have different needs to AI. For example, the people born in US, UK etc. developed countries, they will have high quality of living need in order to improve their daily needs , e.g. more living comfortable feeling. So, non-manual driving cars or robotic driven cars can help them to drive themseleves cars on the roads. These developed countries householders will have much needs to buy non-manual driving cars to replace themselves manual driving cars. They do not like or do not enjoy to drive themselves cars on the roads. Otherwise, the developing countries people, because they are common poor, they need to work to earn to satisfy their daily essential needs, e.g. buying food, paying rent. So, it is common these developing countries poor people , they do not like to buy non-manual driving cars to replace themselves to drive cars on the roads. So, on comfortable living aspect,developed countries rich people , they are common to accept robotics to help them to do any simple or complex tasks . Otherwise, developing countries poor people they are not common to accept robotics to help them to do any simple or complex tasks in society. The reason is that " money spending" problem developing countries poor robotic consumers. But, it does not mean developing countries poor people do not pursue to enjoy to apply robotic to help them to do simple or complex tasks. They are common lazy, they also hope robotic can help them to do any simple or complex tasks in their organizations or houses. If these developing poor countries people can save enough money to buy robotics, or robotic price is cheap, then they will like to spend some money to buy robotic to satisfy their material lives needs.

So,, in the future, it seems that robotics ought influence developed countries people pursue much material lives to satisfy their living needs more than developing countries people in short time. But, when robotic is popular to be accepted to use for anyone. Robotic;s manufacturing number will also increase, then supply number is also influenced to increase. It is possible to influence common every robotic price goes down, then its demand number is global maker. So, when robotic 's price goes down . In general, when developing countries people can save enough money to buy cheaper robotic to use for their living needs. The, many developing countries' people will need robotics to help them to do any simple or complex tasks to householder AI users or organizations AI users . Then, global society will be influenced to change among technology's amazing technological advance, such as robotic makes many people more valuable to their daily lives.

Our society will encounter " pulseless electronic social activity" . it means that our daily activities will need to include robotic's activities to assist our simple or complex active needs. When technology changes, robotic's invention electronic activities satisfy our simple or complex living activities needs, such as non-manual driving activity, hospital non-manual food delivery activity, home non-manual cleaning activity, restaurant non-manual food deliver activity, restaurant non-manual cooking activity, factory non-manual manufacturing or warehouse non-manual goods delivery activity etc.

Hence, robotic will be participated to our daily simple or complex activity to satisfy our lazy needs . I assume that human is lazy animal, human needs some technological thing, such as robotics to help us to do any simple or complex tasks.So, it may say that robotic encourages human's lazy behavior is caused on occurrence in our future society, when robotic is invented to be used to satisfy to different living need aspects. It also means that future robotic may replace computers to help human to do any simple or complex computer tasks. Then, robotics may be applied to replace office workers to do clerical tasks in possible. Our office working environment will be influenced to change robotic clerical workers. Consequently, any working environments will have robotics to be participate to satisfy raising efficiency or improving client service performance or raising productivities needs. Robotics will be needed to any working environments in our society. Talent office or talent restaurant or talent factory or talent warehouse or talent transport tool etc. will be changed to robotic task participation.

In conclusion, our robotic invention may be human's society final change point, our society had experienced from hunting and gathering society to change to pastoral and horticultural society, then from agricultural society changes to industrial societies, till to changes to nowadays postindustrial (information) society. It is unlike the industrial society, this new type of society is not material and manufacture . Rather its basic component is information. Teachers pass on knowledge to students, when lawyers , physicians, bankers , pilots and interior decorators sell their specialized knowledge of law, the body , money to clients. Unlike the factory workers of an industrial society. These individuals don't produce anything. Rather they transmit or use information to provide.

Service that others are willing to pay for such as internet can help any e-commerce to develop online business. Till to biotech society, e.g. in this new biotech. society, the economy will counter on applying and altering genetic structures, both plant and animal to produce food, medicine and material. If there is a ne society, when did it begin ? So, such as robotic invention will bring another new change to our society. Will cloning humans become a reality? Many people object that cloning is immoral, but some will arge the opposite. They will explain why we should leave human reproduction to people who have inferior traits, generic diseases, low IQ, perhaps even the propensity for crime and violence. They will suggest that we select people will finer characteristics, high creative ability, high intelligence, compassion and propensity of peace. Hence, it seems that if future robotics can invented to achieve high IQ, become talent to compare human, such as us. Do you think that it should be our moral obligation to populate society with people like this ? To try to build a society that is better for all, one without terrorism , war, violence. Could this perhaps even be our evolutionary destiny from robotic talent technology. Hence, robotic may help our society to avoid more crime fight, violence, stealing occurrence , they can be such policemen to protect our societies to be more safe to live. It ought mean that robotic can satisfy our living safe need, instead of householders' daily living useful needs and organizations' raising efficiency and improving service performance or raising productivities needs.

Robotic how influences global economic change
Whether robotic invention can bring global economic change to be either improved or better or worse or recession. It depends on many different factoors to influence. I shall indicate some factors as below:
● Encouraging new economic development competitive factor
On new trend in economic development aspect, its invention ought may bring these benefits to our society. Raising social additive utility, technological innovation can bring new economic to competition to our societies or encourage social competition. Then, economics may grow in the social science development view, because robotic;s manufacturing technique can help factories to raise productivities . Then, it encourages manufacturers need to participate competition. For example, when one vehicle manufacture factory decides to apply robotics to assist it to manufacture any cars in the whole manufacturing process. Then, when their cars in the whole manufacture process, when their its worker individual efficiency can raise, performance can be improved. Moreover, its car quality can satisfy to different countries' car buyers. The most importance is that its car productivities number can increase. Thus, it can supply be enough to be sullied to satisfy different countries' car buyers' needs. If its other manufacture competitors do not follow its robotic's participation , so that car manufacture process. Then, they will have much chance to lose their car buyers. So, robotic's manufacture technique to car industry can encourage the global whole car manufacture industries to develop robotic manufacture skills. It encourages whole car manufacture industry will choose robotics to help them to manufacture efficiency and productivities and improve worker's manufacture performance aim. Then, car industry will may increase sale number to increase GDP growth rapidly. So, robotic is intellectural development was perhaps the most significant of this century. It was the explicit negotiation of property rights and transaction costs as

contraints on behaviors.

● How much robotic productivity can raise competition to cause effects of limited competition disadvantage to our society.

Economists had begun to observe the effects in markets of monopolies and of fierce competition. So, when robotic investors own monopolies to manufacture any kinds of robotics or adrtificial intelligence. Then, they will rise robotic's sale price to any business organizational roboticsbuyers or householder buyers, They found that robotics monopolies manufacturers will tend to restrict robotic's limited supplying number to keep high sale prices and profit high in robotic selling market, where there was plenty of competition robotic prices were driven down to the level of costs, profit were low and artificial intelligent robotic output was high.

French economist Anotoine Cournot wanted to find out what happened when there was only few firms had as robotic manufacturers sale is similar to robotic products . In future , robotic manufacturer market, Cournot created his model based on a duopoly of two firms selling indentical spring water to consumers. The two firms are not allowed to turn a cartel by working together, no other firms can enter the industry, because there are no other natural springs and each firm has to decide, how many bottles of water to supply. At this point, each firm is selling the most profitable amount given what the other firm is doing.

Hence, each firm must choose the output that maximizes its profit based on what it thinks that other firms output will be. If firm (A) thinks that firm (B) will produce nothing. Firm (A) will select the low output of a monopolist to maximize the profits. On the other hand, if firm (A) thinks that firm (B) will produce a high output. Firm (A) may choose to produce nothing. Because prices would be too far to make production worthwhile. Due to each firm knows that the other firms' output will affect their own profits. Each firm reacts by selecting its best output given the level of output the other firm chooses (plotted on a reaction curve). The market will be in a Cournot equilibrium where the two reaction curves meet. Consequently, this is low much the firm showed produce, given the competition. Such as robotic manufacturing cases, if two robotic manufacturing firms are not allowed to other firms to enter manufacturing robotic products easily, because they lack robotic's technology to manufacture and each firm has to decide how many robotic products to supply to different countries' robotic organizational buyers and householder buyers both.

The total robotic output of the robotic manufacture industry is the sum of the two robotic manufacture firms' output decisions . Each robotic manufacturer firm must choose the output that maximizes its profit based on what it thinks the other robotic manufactuing firm's output will be. Consequently, they may be unfair to any countries robotic organizational buyers and house holder buyers both. They may give the unreasonable high selling price to by any one robotic product, due to they both control global robotic products number supply and selling price. Consequently, their robotic manufacturing monopolies tended to restrict robotic output to keep high sale prices and profit high to global robotic organizations and householders buyers both. It is very unfair to global robotic consumers. So, however, future when economic is recession, global robotic's sale price will not be influenced to go down easily, due to these two robotic manufacturing monopolies companies control global robotic product manufacturer market. Future robotic consumers will need to pay unreasonable high price to buy any kinds of robotic products, if these are only two robotic manufacturers own monopolies to control global robotic supply output number ans sale price leve. It is one case to explain unfair robotic manufacturers' competition to bring global future unreasonable robotic high sale price as well as limited supply number disadvantages to any countries' robotic to consumers.

So, in game theory, future robotic manufacturers number must need to above at least two firms, even more than ten firms when global has many robotic buyers number will increase. Consequently, when economic recession occurs, robotic's price will climb up. It will influence many robotic buyers can not buy any kinds of robotic product to help them to raise efficiency or productivities if many factories have need, but they can not buy any robotic to assist them to workers to raise productivities or efficiency. Then, their productivities number can not satisfy consumers' needs. Consequently, GDP will also influenced to go down. Because robotic will be future manufactur industry's important asset, they may help any manufacturers to raise productivities in long time. If many manufacturers have enough money to buy robotic to assist workers to manufacture any products. Then, global product export number will redice. So, robotic manufacturer market can not be monopolies to control by at least two firms. They will influence global manufacturing industry export can not increse to satisfy consumers needs easily. Then, economic recession will be more serious indeed.

In conclusion, future robotic manufacture market will influence economic recession or not. It depends on a system of free robotic manufacturing market is needed to stable. Because when shortages of robotic supply in own area of the economy create surplues of supply. Either where there are robotic supply shortages, so prices rise or when these are robotic supply surplues prices fall. When price riase, global robotic demand falls and robotic supply rises, aims to eliminating shortageto robotic or robotic prices fall, global robotic demand rises, and robotic supply falls aims to eliminating surplus to robotic. Consequently, they will cause that economics is as a whole tend towards equilibrium as long as they are free to do so. Also , a system of free robotic manufacture market is needed to stable, global robotic sale price is to be more reasonable and fair and output supply number to robotic organization and housholder consumers in order to satisfy raising efficiency or improving productivity or performance aim to factories organizations. Hence, robotic supply output number and sale price will have direct relationship to influence future GDP growth or recession.

● How and why robotic brings long time intellectural development to global factories ?

Rarely, in any science, has a new development turned so rapidly influence global different industries aspects, such as robotic technological development can influence different industries aspect to bring more intelligent and creature attributies. The economic of property and rights of robotic has major change in the direction of economic thinking has to do with the purpose or intent or research to encourage global robotic scientists can compete to cooperate to achieve the more advanced or intellectural of any kinds or functions to different robotic's industries uses.

Whereas, earlier economists began to believe that cooperative competition work bring more creative ability more than non-cooperative competition. So, whan different professional robotic scientists can cooperate to work together, they will raise " brain storm" creative ability to continue to create non-discovered or non-reserch future robotic products. So, nowadays, our robotic products do not only to limit to reash the final invention number. In the future, economists had predicted our future society ought have many new kinds or new functions of robotics new products are invented to satisfy robotic consumers different needs, e.g. applying to space or earth or ocean non manual exploration science tasks aspects, non pilot driving flying aspect, hospital medical non manual surgeon or non manual patient food delivery aspects. Then, due to future our society's different industries aspects can be participated by robotics to help to cooperate to achieve any mission in oder to achieve any reasearchs more successful. Thus, future robotics' role are not only to do complex or simple tasks for manufacturers or householders. They may be used for any scientists to participate to achieve any important research missions more successful. Thus, future robotics will be applied for scientists in order to assist them to achieve any important research missions more successful. For example, robotic is applied to garment and toy industries. It can bring more advantages to factory works and manufacturers. Pieceworkers may work either in a factory where space and tools are provided or at home using their own equipment, before none any robotic's participation to pieceworkers' tasks . But when robotic invention, home factory robotic's coordination of activities is improved when all workers perform under one tool supplementing with work sent out to home craftsman only at times of people loads. So, robotics help factory workers to reduce workload. Moreover, pieceworkers in factories are often assigned specific machines to avoid careless use random rotation, and fast workers are often assigned the better equipment. But when robotic's participation to their tasks. However, foolish and clever workers must give advantages , robotics can assist foolish workers to raise efficiency as well as clever workers can be improved their productivities number predictably. Piece rate work which do not require the use of heavy machinery, it tends to apply robotic to be produced in a factory. So, home workers do not need. They do not need machinery in a home, dangerous to children and requires repair, it may not also be so costly that few home workers woud willingly invest without assurance of long term use. When robotic can be replaced to any home or factory machine.

So, robotic can assist foolish and clever workers to raise management productivities more than traditional simple machine. Thus, future management ought make clear judgement whether whom is clever or foolish workers when they need to cooperate to robotics to work together. Also, they may give more reasonable wage to the worker, if the worker can cooperate to robotic to raise more productivites number. Then, he ought need to give bonus , instead of basic piece number wage calculation method. Otherwise, if the worker can nor improve his productive performane after ne needs to cooperate with robotic. Then, he must need time to learn how to cooperate to robotic in order to adapt together factory working environment. So, new robotic's participation to any factory, every worker will need time to adapt how to cooperation with its change. The bonus paid system will depend on whom can adapt to cooperate with robotic in order to achieve the most rapid raising efficiency or improving productivities perform objective. Thus, in economic view , robotic's factory participative tasks, which can assist worker's cooperation more effectively. Consequently, when one factory all workers can adapt to cooperate with robotic to work together . The factory's productivities number must be raised in long time. Consequently, the factory's worker efficiency and productivity number must be improved , due to robotic can improve its manufacturing skills to be upgrade absolutely. Also, factory management can decide advantages result to determining piece wage rates , then would be possible if contributes were only be measured by machine . When, robotic's participation to every clever or foolish worker tasks, it can influence their performance to be accepted or rejected more easily . So, in general, foolish workers need long time to learn how to cooperate with robotic to work together, tey must not earn bonus or increase piece wage easily in short time. Otherwise, clever worker can adapt how to cooperate with robotic to work. So, their piece productivities number must increase in short time. So, bonus or increasing piece wage paid method may be evaluated to compensate to every workers more fair in the factory . It is robotic's factory participation to worker individual tasks economic benefit to any future factories manuacturing environment.

● How can robotic help manufacturers to raise productivitied or improve efficiency?

In modern economic view, robotic's participation to worker tasks, it ought achieve better productivites number. We need to make choice because productive resources are scare. Hence, in factory environment, manufacturing resources ought only include workers, traditional old machines and advance robotic. If the factory expects to achieve the most effective productivites. When they have robotic choice to be productive resources. Therefore, they make robotic productive resources, they may ask these questions: Can robotic assist economy growing or stagnant?

Growth means greater output and potentially higher levels of living for a society; stagnation removes that possibility for improvement. IS a society using its productive resources fully and efficiently? Anything less will mean unemployment of people, machine and other productive agents? For whom to produce? It concerns that distribution of the output, who in a particular society will get the goods and services that are produced? How to produce? such as factory choice to productive resources case, factory may still choose machine and worker together production or workers only productin or robotic only production or robotic and workers together productive method. It concerns the methods that a society can use to undertake its production. Usually, an item can be produced, with various different techniques , a lot of labor and only a few machines as a lot of labor and only a few robotics , or few labours and a lot of robotics , or a lot of machinery and very few workers. What to produce? Which goods among the endless possibilities will a society decide upon, an in what quantity? What decision-making process will be used to arrive at the answer?

So, in microeconomics, manufacturers consider how to make industrial productive decision in order. It concerns how resources are allocated, such as workers and/or machine and robotic's factory managers. However, microeconomic takes how that it is divided by product, how to minimize the resources, such as workers number nnd without machine, when robotics can replace machine to assist workers to raise productivities and improve efficiencies in any factory environment, but on the same time, in macroeconomic view, when robotic participation to few workers tasks. It will also increase high unemployment or stagnating growth , due to many factory workers lose their tasks, due to robotics may help them to raise productivities.So, workers ' roles will be assistants, but robotics will be the main important actor to produce and products in the factories.

● Why does production possibilities curve may explain why robotic participation may assist few workers to raise productivities in factories ?

One simple model, known as the production possibilities curve, is very helpful to explain traditional machine and workers cooperation can not produce more products more than robotics and workers cooperation, how choices must be made among scarce economic alternatives. Supposing a vehicle manufacturing factory , factory area/floor size is fixed, the factory supply of tools can only choose either machine or robotic altered. So, the factory can not choose both productive resources to assist workers to produce any vehicels, and th number of working hours can not increase, but many decrease. There is not extra money supply to consider . Hence, if the factory sells all with resource scarce limited tools, either robotic or machine choice, worker working time can be increased, but may decrease and managerial worker ability can not improve, because managers number can not increase, may only decrease.

If the factory expects to raise vehicle productive number, it only may choose to apply robotic to replace machine. Robotic can bring cost reducing advantage in long term, when the foolish workers can not be trained to apply robotic to cooperate to raise vehicle productivities number. the talent workers can be trained to raise vehicle productivites number. Even, when some talent managers can be trained to supervise many robotic and workers to work together efficiently. Then, the factory may reduce the foolish managers and foolish workers. It 's whole vehicle productivities number may still be raised, when trained talent workers and managers can adapt to work with robotics to raise their productivities number in long time.

It is based to explain why robotic can help workers to raise productivities in this productive possibilities curve. When the factory needs to manufacture two kinds of unique vehicles. f this factory still choose machine and workers to manufacture the (A)kind of vehicles and the (B) kind of vehicles . It can manufacture the maximum (A) knid of number vehicles is 20 pieces as well as the maximum (B) kind of number vehicles is 20 pieces every hours. Otherwise, if this factory changes productive resource to apply robotics to replaced machine and foolish workers to manufacture the kind (A) of vehicles, the kind of (A) vehicles maximum number is 40 pieces as well as the kind of (B) vehicles maximum number is 40 vehicles also every hour.

The kind of maximum (A) and (B) vehicles number manufacturing effect per hour, shows production level higher than actually be attained and more efficiency, when the factory applies effectively the rpbotics and trained talent workers and trained talent managers resources to replace the traditional old machines and the foolish workers resources to manufacture the both kinds of (A) and (B) unique vehicles in this factory.

Although, this factory's factory floor size can not increase and money is limited . So, it has only twenty productive resource machine number can not increase to buy more twenty robotic to replace them,even robotic's number may be reduced, as well as it has fifty workers and five factory manager number, it can not increase more than these number. But due to when managers and workers can be trained to proficient to know how to control any one of these ten only robotics to manufacture the kind (A) and kind (B) unique vehicles. Then, this factory's robotic purchase expenditure must be decreased to only ten number, even when some trained workers can be traned to be talent to proficient how to shorten time manufcture every kind (A) an kind (B) unuqie vehicels from the maximum number 20 pieces to (A) and 20 pieces to (B) vehicles per hour to the maximum number 40 pieces to (A) and 40 piece to (B) vehicles per hour.

Thenm this factory can attempt to reduce the foolish workers and foolish managers umber and ot only employ the talent workers and managers to cooperate with ten only robotics number, when these talent workers and managers can ensure to know hoew to control these ten robotic together in order to achieve the maximum productivites kind (A) 40 piece and kind (B) 40 piece every hour effort in possibility.

In this both (A) and (B) unique vehicle manufacture case, this simple robotic production possible productive curve represents an important modern economics. The prdocutive cost is property defined as opportunity cost . This factory only may choose two methods ot productive resources. Either is lot clever and foolish workers and managers number and lot machine number or few worker number (only trained) clever workers and few robotics number. This factory have no money costs of production , when it sells all machines to buy few robotic number, even it can save money if robot purchase cost is less than all machine selling cost. Moreover, the factory will only dismiss the low skilled ot inefficient workers and the low managerial abilities managers to reduce salary expenditure when they can not be trained to proficient to control any one robotic to raise the both kinds (A) and (B) vehicles productivites number for a period. For example, after three months training time, their productivities number to kind (A) and (B) vehicles can not be increased absolutely.

Thus, production possibilities curve can explain why this factory ought choose to decide to sell its all machines and buy robotics to replace them in order to participate to the only trained talent workers and manager teams to cooperate to concentrate on onlymanufacturing the both (A) and (B) vehicle number per hour and in order to achieve improving performance, raising both kinds unique (A) and (B) vehicles productivities and efficiency aim.

Must Developed And Developing Countries Need Artificial Intelligent To Replace Human Job

Must developed and developing countries need artificial intelligent development? If one developed country, e.g. US, UK , Japan , Singapore it does not continue to develop artificial intelligence, robotic, then what disadvantges or weaknesses , it will encounter to compare when it chooses to continue to develop this artificial intelligent technology in society. If one developing country, e.g. China, Korea, Taiwan, it does not continue to develop artificial intelligence, robotic, then what disadantages or weaknesses, it will also encounter to compare when it chooses to continue to develop this artificial intelligent technology in in society. I shall explan the reasons why the results may cause to either the developed country, or the developing country as below:

● How AI help developing countries to communication and agriculture and learning and medical delivery development

Why can AI help developing countries ? Drones that pick inaccessible crops and mobile phones that give medical advice are two of the ways AI can transform life in the developing world. Artificial intelligence (AI) may improve the lives of the world's poor, the technology needed to revolutionise inefficient, ineffective food and healthcare systems in developing countries is well. For example, in low-income areas, agriculture and healthcare are two critical ecosystems that we can apply AI to immediately; this is not the far future, or even in five years.

Artificial intelligence (AI) has seeped into the daily lives of people in the developed world. From virtual assistants to recommendation engines, AI is in the news, our homes and offices. There is a lot of potential in terms of AI usage, especially in humanitarian areas. The impact could have a multiplier effect in developing countries, where resources are limited.

Emergency Response to developing countries' earthquake natural damage suddence occurrence predicting

AI and machine learning are still finding importance in emerging markets, but certain applications have emerged and are now widely used. For instance, predictive models for disaster relief enable first responders to automatically analyze large-scale behavior and movement through multiple sources of data including social media platforms, web forums, news sources, etc. Based on collected data, responders can scale reconstruction efforts and distribute supplies in a timely manner.

Why and how AI can assist farmers to predict when the earthquake occurs suddenly in order to avoid or reduce the natural damage to their agriculture productive number loss. For example, In 2015, when a major earthquake hit Nepal, more than 8 million people were affected. During the aftermath, drones were used to map and assess the destruction and speed up the rescue mission. The town of Sankhu, situated about 20 kilometers northeast of Kathmandu, was among the highly affected locations. In May 2018, my company Fusemachines and GeoSpatial Systems partnered with Sankhu's city officials to use drones and artificial intelligence in an effort to automatically estimate the reconstruction need. After processing data accumulated from a drone-powered aerial mapping of the region, the team fed this data to advanced machine learning algorithms. Combining drone imagery, digital mapping and machine learning, the team configured region modeling and infrastructure development with higher accuracy. Another organization known as One Concern, a California-based startup, has created a predictive AI program called Seismic Concern to accurately predict seism and is also working on solutions for wildfires, floods and hurricanes.

Smart AI Agriculture

Another application of AI in developing countries is smart agriculture. Farmers monitor crops more effectively and make better predictions on planting, weeding and harvesting using AI tools. It can also be used to analyze one plant at a time and add pesticides only to infected plants and trees instead of spraying pesticides across large swaths of crops. One California-based tech company is an example of this use of AI. So, the developing countries farmers in rural parts of India are also using AI to increase yields through better access to information about the farming season than they would normally have. Technology-enabled process automation offers the agribusiness industry the chance for remarkable growth -- not only in developed countries but around the world. There's a unique opportunity to increase yields, cut down labor costs and improve people's health.

Medicine Delivery to developing countries' patients urgent need

Companies are also leveraging AI to improve access to health care in some of the most remote areas of the world. In Rwanda, for example, Zipline is using drones to deliver medical supplies and blood to hospitals and clinics that are difficult to access by car. This has dramatically impacted people living in remote parts of the country because they are able to get medical help when needed. The drone system in Rwanda has also helped reduce waste of blood by 95%, as noted by Zipline. One Concern has created an AI program called Seismic Concern that accurately predicts seismic events and is also working on solutions for floods, wildfires and hurricanes. The medical field may actually benefit the most from emerging technologies in developing countries.

Assistance to reduce teaching work workload or psychological pressure to teachers in developing countries' schools

Another vital area benefiting from innovative technologies like AI is education. Advanced technologies can enhance how we learn, teach and perform tasks. In most developing countries, schools lack experienced teachers and resources to enhance students' knowledge. As a result, many students still have to walk long distances to get to the nearest school, which has created education gaps, especially in rural areas. AI tools such as personalized learning assistants can simplify learning by making tutoring services and learning materials accessible to all students, wherever they are. Machines can be automated to help students learn basic concepts without a tutor, which companies like Carnegie Learning are working on. This would allow students to learn at any time from anywhere. With AI, education is made easy and accessible to more people.

The initial usage of AI in developing countries has been at a micro level -- solving small, specific problems in a defined industry. As machine learning advances and there is a higher utilization of AI, we will see more complex issues being targeted and resolved. When duly adopted, AI can positively impact future developing countries people everyday lives not just in disaster intervention, education, health care and agriculture but can also help in mitigating poverty, malnutrition and pollution. Especially, in developing nations, to leverage AI's true potential and create a snowball effect. Startups are defining a holistic and humanitarian approach to building more sophisticated, AI-ready societies. Stakeholders in the AI landscape should understand the strengths and nuances of the developing world as well as the limitations of AI and create localized solutions and applications.

Why does smart phone help developing countries communication ?

Internet Seen as Positive Influence on Education but Negative on Morality in Emerging and Developing Nations. Internet access differs substantially across the 32 emerging and developing countries polled, with the lowest rates of internet use in South Asian and sub-Saharan African nations. Within countries, computer owners, young people, the well-educated, the wealthy and those with English language ability are much more likely to access the internet than their counterparts. To access the internet, people increasingly use smartphones rather than more cumbersome fixed landline connections and computers. Around the world, both smartphones and basic-feature phones alike are used for sending messages and taking pictures.

In fact, many developing countries young people, students are popular to use smart phones for internet usage aim, instead of communication. Moreover, many developing countries working people are also popular to use smart phones for any working usage in their working time , even non working time any time. So, smart phones (AI) phones will be important communication or leisure tools to developing countries people in the future. Unless, it is one day, scientists can develop another new communication tool to replace smart phones. So, artificial intelligence will be important to influence developing countries people , how to improve or bring positive learning attitudes to students in their daily learnnng lifes. as well as how to raise developing countries people, how to raise working people efficiency or improve performace in their daily working lifes. So, AI may bring positive learning or working attitudes to developing countries working people and students both.

The Positive Impact of Mass Media in Developing Countries

Radio, newspapers, television, Internet, social media, etc., all of these are forms of mass media. Each of these outlets has the capability of bringing information to thousands of people with one device. While in some communities it is easy to take advantage of these communication outlets such as television and Internet access, not everyone has access to such outlets. Radio is one of the most common forms of mass media in developing countries because it's affordable and uses less electricity than many other forms of mass media, but only approximately 75 percent of people in developing countries have access to a radio, and roughly 77 percent of people in rural areas have access to electricity.

For developing countries that have implemented forms of mass media in their communities, there have been numerous positive outcomes are influenced to impact developing countries mass media by artificial intelligence as below:

When AI is participated to developing countries mass media, it can influence any radio, television audiences raise more attention to each other through social media platforms such as Facebook and Twitter and create, organize and initiate street protests and campaigns. Furthermore, having access to social media in developing countries, people are able to connect to those that they usually wouldn't have the chance to talk to. Moreover, AI Provides educational opportunities- In many countries, the division between local and national languages as well as issues of literacy can make communication difficult. With the use of mass media, a bridge can be built between these two gaps. In India, there is a radio station that provides information in local languages and respects local culture and traditions. One of the main ways is to create public awareness of what is going on with businesses and government officials. The media plays an important role in giving people the opportunity to act against injustice, oppression and misdeeds that they otherwise wouldn't know about. Information on available healthcare, a mass radio broadcast was sent out encouraging parents to seek treatment at local healthcare facilities for their sick children. With this mass outreach on healthcare, the encouragement of people to take their children to healthcare facilities saved thousands of lives. This easy way of encouraging others and bringing awareness about certain diseases was made possible through a simple radio broadcast. Finally, when AI is particiapted to media, it may bring many social issues to life that otherwise would remain unknown to many people. In developing countries and communities like Burkina Faso, when the radio broadcast was released about malaria, diarrhea and pneumonia, people were educated and moved to action and knew to take their children to healthcare facilities for preventative care. As it is seen, having access to different media outlets is vital for those in developing countries. Here are three ways that those in developing countries can implement mass media to help their people and communities.

When AI is participated to any internet radio or internet newspaper mass online listening or reading channel. It can provide online radios or newspapers in public places- By providing online radios and newspapers in public areas it gives community members to access news, information and emergency warnings. Even though radios can be on the cheaper side, there are still many people that can't afford to have a radio in their home. By providing one in a local place, not only would it better educate the community members but also it will bring the community together. So, it can make media outlets a two-way platform- Creating a two-way platform between the community and those who are behind the radio stations, newspapers or broadcasts makes the community feel involved and that their voices are being heard. An organization called Soul City in sub-Saharan Africa is showing how well two-way platforms work by engaging their listeners and having them contribute thoughts and ideas about complex issues. Because developing countries radio listening audiences or newspaper readers are popular to accept computer online radio listening channel or online newspaper reading channel to replace traditional paper newspapers or radio machines. So, AI may raise their listening news or reading news leisure feeling from online mass media channel in the future.

● Why do developed countries need to develop AI
Artificial intelligence, or AI, is driving massive shifts across the globe, and every day more questions arise. What impact will AI have on the workforce and how can we prepare for it? How can we encourage economy-boosting

and job-creating technologies? How can we ensure that AI will be implemented ethically and with minimal bias? How will society benefit? For developed country, such as US example. None of the US, Israel and Russia have a formal national AI policy yet. Private sector companies such as Google, Amazon and Apple and the US department of defence are driving the bulk of AI investment in the United States. Though Israel does not have a specific policy, it is keenly focused on AI and has seen the number of AI start-ups triple since 2014.

Developed country may learn whether what weakness it is lacking when it does not continue to develop AI from one another developed country. Which countries are approaching AI most effectively, and to what degree is there opportunity for greater international collaboration? It may be too early to tell; however, when analyzing the best practices of existing national AI policies, there is much that can be learned. These are the specific areas to consider. When one developed country continue to develop or research AI, it may bring these benefits as below:

On gathering Data aspect, from self-driving vehicles to smart cities, data is the driver behind AI. Innovation in the United States is limited without a national strategy that answers questions about protocol and ownership. France and Denmark, on the other hand, are opening government data. France is hosting troves of centrally collected public and private data that it plans to make available as part of its strategy. Conversely, by taking a restrictive position on issues of data collection (as indicated by the implementation of General Data Protection Regulation), the EU is putting manufacturers and software designers at a disadvantage while balancing the demand for privacy. On raising technologica talent aspect, the demand for AI talent far outweighs the available supply. As a result, almost every nation's strategy addresses talent development. Canada's AI strategy is distinct in that it primarily focuses on research and talent strategy. The country boasts AI degree programmes and is building a $127 million research facility in Toronto. Companies like Facebook and my own company, Uptake, are investing in Canada to access this talent pool. On AI legal technological innovation aspect, a whole host of legal questions swirl around AI. The country is developing a bill for AI liability that will be ready in March 2019. The government hopes the legal framework will attract investors by providing a simple, comprehensive guideline to enable the broad use of AI systems. So, when the developed country applied AI technology to assist any lawyers to work, then AI can help them to reduce the workload to draft any legal documents more easier. So, any developed countries lawyers' draft legal documents time must reduce if the developed countries lawyers accept to apply AI to assist their legal works. One of the great promises of AI is its potential for improving quality of life. But without the right planning and oversight, we risk exacerbating problems of inequality or marginalizing groups of people. As an example, India's AI strategy is focused on leveraging the technology not only for economic growth, but also for social inclusion.

AI may bring what benefits to developed countries
From SIRI to self-driving cars, artificial intelligence (AI) is progressing rapidly. While science fiction often portrays AI as robots with human-like characteristics, AI can encompass anything from Google's search algorithms to IBM's Watson to autonomous weapons. Artificial intelligence today is properly known as narrow AI (or weak AI), in that it is designed to perform a narrow task (e.g. only facial recognition or only internet searches or only driving a car). However, the long-term goal of many researchers is to create general AI (AGI or strong AI). While narrow AI may outperform humans at whatever its specific task is, like playing chess or solving equations, AGI would outperform humans at nearly every cognitive task.
Why research AI safety? Would AI bring war when AI is continued to develop by developed countries? In the near term, the goal of keeping AI's impact on society beneficial motivates research in many areas, from economics and law to technical topics such as verification, validity, security and control. Whereas it may be little more than a minor nuisance if your laptop crashes or gets hacked, it becomes all the more important that an AI system does what you want it to do if it controls your car, your airplane, your pacemaker, your automated trading system or your power grid. Another short-term challenge is preventing a devastating arms race in lethal autonomous weapons.
In the long term, an important question is what will happen if the quest for strong AI succeeds and an AI system becomes better than humans at all cognitive tasks. As pointed out by I.J. Good in 1965, designing smarter AI systems is itself a cognitive task. Such a system could potentially undergo recursive self-improvement, triggering an intelligence explosion leaving human intellect far behind. By inventing revolutionary new technologies, such a superintelligence might help us eradicate war, disease, and poverty, and so the creation of strong AI might be the biggest event in human history. Some experts have expressed concern, though, that it might also

be the last, unless we learn to align the goals of the AI with ours before it becomes superintelligent.

There are some who question whether strong AI will ever be achieved, and others who insist that the creation of superintelligent AI is guaranteed to be beneficial. At FLI we recognize both of these possibilities, but also recognize the potential for an artificial intelligence system to intentionally or unintentionally cause great harm. We believe research today will help us better prepare for and prevent such potentially negative consequences in the future, thus enjoying the benefits of AI while avoiding pitfalls.

How can AI be dangerous when developed countries continue to develop AI to become weapon to replace soldiers?

Most researchers agree that a superintelligent AI is unlikely to exhibit human emotions like love or hate, and that there is no reason to expect AI to become intentionally benevolent or malevolent. Instead, when considering how AI might become a risk, experts think two scenarios most likely:

The AI is programmed to do something devastating: Autonomous weapons are artificial intelligence systems that are programmed to kill. In the hands of the wrong person, these weapons could easily cause mass casualties. Moreover, an AI arms race could inadvertently lead to an AI war that also results in mass casualties. To avoid being thwarted by the enemy, these weapons would be designed to be extremely difficult to simply "turn off," so humans could plausibly lose control of such a situation. This risk is one that's present even with narrow AI, but grows as levels of AI intelligence and autonomy increase.

The AI is programmed to do something beneficial, but it develops a destructive method for achieving its goal: This can happen whenever we fail to fully align the AI's goals with ours, which is strikingly difficult. If you ask an obedient intelligent car to take you to the airport as fast as possible, it might get you there chased by helicopters and covered in vomit, doing not what you wanted but literally what you asked for. If a superintelligent system is tasked with a ambitious geoengineering project, it might wreak havoc with our ecosystem as a side effect, and view human attempts to stop it as a threat to be met. So, a super-intelligent AI will be extremely good at accomplishing its goals, and if those goals aren't aligned with ours, we have a problem. You're probably not an evil ant-hater who steps on ants out of malice, but if you're in charge of a hydroelectric green energy project and there's an anthill in the region to be flooded, too bad for the ants. A key goal of AI safety research is to never place humanity in the position of those ants.

Why the recent interest in AI safety ?

Stephen Hawking, Elon Musk, Steve Wozniak, Bill Gates, and many other big names in science and technology have recently expressed concern in the media and via open letters about the risks posed by AI, joined by many leading AI researchers. The idea that the quest for strong AI would ultimately succeed was long thought of as science fiction, centuries or more away. However, thanks to recent breakthroughs, many AI milestones, which experts viewed as decades away merely five years ago, have now been reached, making many experts take seriously the possibility of superintelligence in our lifetime. While some experts still guess that human-level AI is centuries away, most AI researches at the 2015 Puerto Rico Conference guessed that it would happen before 2060. Since it may take decades to complete the required safety research, it is prudent to start it now.

Because AI has the potential to become more intelligent than any human, we have no surprise way of predicting how it will behave. We can't use past technological developments as much of a basis because we've never created anything that has the ability to, wittingly or unwittingly, outsmart us. The best example of what we could face may be our own evolution. People now control the planet, not because we're the strongest, fastest or biggest, but because we're the smartest. If we're no longer the smartest, are we assured to remain in control?

A captivating conversation is taking place about the future of artificial intelligence and what it will/should mean for humanity. There are fascinating controversies where the world's leading experts disagree, such as: AI's future impact on the job market; if/when human-level AI will be developed; whether this will lead to an intelligence explosion; and whether this is something we should welcome or fear. But there are also many examples of of boring pseudo-controversies caused by people misunderstanding and talking past each other. When one developed country continue to develop AI, can itself country's all factories workers will lose jobs, due to AI can replace them to do simple works in factories, or any public transport drivers, e.g. bus drivers, ferry , tram, train drivers, they will lose jobs, when AI (non manual driving drivers) can replace all public transport drivers. So, some occupations will lose if developed countries continue to develop or research AI to replace human to do some simple jobs, such as some cooking jobs can be done by AI. So, it is possible that future cookers won't be needed, because AI cooking skills may be better than them to cook any good taste chinese or western food in restaurants. If you drive down the road, you have a subjective experience of colors, sounds, etc. But does a self-driving car have a subjective experience? Does it feel like anything at all to be a self-driving car? Although this mystery of consciousness is interesting in its own right, it's irrelevant to AI risk. If you get struck by a driverless car, it makes no difference to you whether it subjectively feels conscious. In the same way, what will affect us humans is what superintelligent AI does, not how it subjectively feels.

In fact, AI may be make any brokers jobs in financial market. the main concern of the beneficial-AI movement isn't with robots but with intelligence itself: specifically, intelligence whose goals are misaligned with ours. To cause us trouble, such misaligned superhuman intelligence needs no robotic body, merely an internet connection – this may enable outsmarting financial markets, out-inventing human researchers, out-manipulating human leaders, and developing weapons we cannot even understand. Even if building robots were physically impossible, a super-intelligent and super-wealthy AI could easily pay or manipulate many humans to unwittingly do its bidding. So, future brokers will be replaced by AI, when AI can be made to own financial brokers' analytical mind to make more accurate whether the share price will rise up or fall down to compare human financial brokers' analytical mind. The robot misconception is related to the myth that machines can't control humans. Intelligence enables control: humans control tigers not because we are stronger, but because we are smarter. This means that if we cede our position as smartest on our planet, it's possible that we might also cede control.

Not wasting time on the above-mentioned misconceptions lets us focus on true and interesting controversies where even the experts disagree. What sort of future do you want? Should we develop lethal autonomous weapons? What would you like to happen with job automation? What career advice would you give today's kids? Do you prefer new jobs replacing the old ones, or a jobless society where everyone enjoys a life of leisure and machine-produced wealth? Further down the road, would you like us to create superintelligent life and spread it through our cosmos? Will we control intelligent machines or will they control us? Will intelligent machines replace us, coexist with us, or merge with us? What will it mean to be human in the age of artificial intelligence?

Why do developed countries people need AI ?

Why do we assume that AI will require more and more physical space and more power when human intelligence continuously manages to miniaturize and reduce power consumption of its devices. How low the power needs and how small will the machines be by the time quantum computing becomes reality? Why do we assume that AI will exist as independent machines? If so, and the AI is able to improve its Intelligence by reprogramming itself, will machines driven by slower processors feel threatened, not by mere stupid humans, but by machines with faster processors? What would drive machines to reproduce themselves when there is no biological incentive, pressure or need to do so?

Who says superior AI will need or want to have a physical existence when an immaterial AI could evolve and preserve itself better from external dangers. What will happen if AI developed by competing ideologies, liberalism vs communism, reach maturity at the same time, will they fight for hegemony by trying to destroy each other physically and/or virtually. If AI is programmed to believe in God, and competing AI emerges programmed by muslims, christians or jews, how are the different AI's going to make sense of the different religious beliefs, are we going to have AI religious wars? What if the "powers that be" greatest fear is the emergence of a super AI that police's and rationalizes the distribution of wealth and food. A friendly super AI that is programmed to help humanity by, enforcing the declaration of Human Rights (the US is the only industrialized country that to this day has not signed this declaration) ending corruption and racism and protecting the environment.Most benefits of civilization stem from intelligence, so how can we enhance these benefits with artificial intelligence without being replaced on the job market and perhaps altogether?

Key to the process of machine learning are neural networks. These are brain-inspired networks of interconnected layers of algorithms, called neurons, that feed data into each other, and which can be trained to carry out specific tasks by modifying the importance attributed to input data as it passes between the layers. During training of these neural networks, the weights attached to different inputs will continue to be varied until the output from the neural network is very close to what is desired, at which point the network will have 'learned' how to carry out a particular task. A subset of machine learning is deep learning, where neural networks are expanded into sprawling networks with a huge number of layers that are trained using massive amounts of data. It is these deep neural networks that have fuelled the current leap forward in the ability of computers to carry out task like speech recognition and computer vision.

In conclusion, when developed countries continue to develop AI, it may bring positive advantages to bring raising productivies, or efficiencies, but it may also raise unemployment ratio to any low skill or low knowledge jobs in ther societies. However, human future society will need to change to be better to raise our living standard. But AI is one kind the best choice tool to achieve this aim in our future, so I agree developed countries continue to develop or research AI to be the super -human machine.

Reference

A. Castano et. al. " Automatic detection of dust devils and clouds at Mars" Machine vision and applications, Oct. 2008, vol. 19, no 5-6, pp. 467-482.

Accenture, " Why artificial intelligence is the future of growth"(2017) <http://www.accenture.com/us-en/insight-a   rtificial-intelligence-future-growth>.

D. Schedidt , Unmanned Air Vehicle Command And Control, Handbook Of Unmanned Air Vehicles, Springer-Verlag, 2014. Facebook (AI) Research Available at https://research.facebook.com/ai, research at google, machine intelligence available at

http://research.google.com/pubs/machineintellige nce.html; micro soft research-machine learning and artificial intelligence available at <http://research.microsoft.com/en-us/research- areas/machine-learning-ai.aspx>.

International Federation Of Robotics, 2016. IFR press release world robotics report. IFR, org . 29 Sept. Accessed Feb. 01, 2017. http://www.ifr.org/news/ifr-press-release/world-robitics   report -2016-8321.

K, Fedra , "GIS and environmental modelling" in environmental modelling with GIS, edited by M.F. Goodchild.B.O. Parks and L.T. Steyaert, Oxford University press, pp. 35-50, 1994.

Keynes, J.M. (1933). Economic possibilities for our grandchildren (1930). Essays in persuasion, pp.358-73.

Mckinsey & Company (2013, May). Disruptive technologies: Advices that will transform life, business and the global economy , USA.

Ministry of economy, trade and industry, Japan, 2015, Japan's robot strategy. Ministry of economy, trade and industry.

Ray Kurzweil , The age of spiritual machines (1999) is cited numerously through this chapter: Kurzweilai.net http://www.kurzweilai.net

Rich, Elaine & Knight, Kevin, Artificial Intelligence Second Edition, 1991, New York; Mc-Graw-Hill.

Artificial intelligence bank service working environment
Focus on outcomes not technology.Artificial Intelligence: Waiting to be unleashed? The Insider Column - When Digital Transformation misses. Are you meeting the demands of the new digital consumer? Will your legacy mindset compromise your digital competitiveness? Can artificial intelligence create online remote office new business service market in global ?
The Future of Artificial Intelligence In The Workplace:
Is AI going to displace workers or come as a benefit to them?
Is AI going to displace workers or come as a benefit to them? Getty
Smart technologies aren't just changing our homes; they're edging their way into their numerous industries and are disrupting the workplace. Artificial Intelligence (AI) has the potential to improve productivity, efficiency and accuracy across an organization – but is this entirely beneficial? Many fear that the rise of AI will lead to machines and robots replacing human workers and view this progression in technology as threat rather than a tool to better ourselves.

With AI continuing to be a prominent online office service business to replace human actual office working environment, businesses need to realize that self-learning and black-box capabilities are not the panacea. Many organisations are already beginning to see the incredible capabilities of AI, using these advantages to enhance human intelligence and gain real value from their data. As there is increasing evidence demonstrating the benefits of intelligent systems, more decision-makers in the boardroom are gaining a better understanding of what AI can really offer. Research conducted by EY explains "organizations enabling AI at the enterprise level are increasing operational efficiency, making faster, more informed decisions and innovating new products and services." Can articial intelligent technology create remote office working environment to replace our traditional actual office work environment ? Can we do not need to go to office to work , when any office staffs ,e.g. managers, clerk, etc. they can apply artificial intelligent technology and online technology to work at home, such as remote office working environment ?

The first companies employing AI systems across the board will gain competitive advantage, reduce cost of operations and remove head counts. Whilst this may be a positive from a business perspective, it is obvious why this a worry for those working in roles at risk of displacement. The introduction of these technologies will likely trigger an issue with unions and job security due to the substantial operational changes. Although AI will affect every sector in some way, not every job is at equal risk. PwC predicts a relatively low displacement of jobs (around 3%) in the first wave of automation, but this could dramatically increase up to 30% by the mid-2030's. Occupations within the transport industry could potentially be at much greater risk, whereas jobs requiring social, emotional and literary abilities are at the lowest risk of displacement.

A positive future with artificial intelligence to bring remote online office working environment chance:

Many businesses and individuals are optimistic that this AI-driven shift in the workplace will result in more jobs being created than lost. As we develop innovative technologies, AI will have a positive impact on our economy by creating jobs that require the skill set to implement new systems. 80% of respondents in the EY survey said it was the lack of these skills that was the biggest challenge when employing AI programs.

It is likely that artificial intelligence will soon replace jobs involving repetitive or basic problem-solving tasks, and even go beyond current human capability. AI systems will be making decisions instead of humans in industrial settings, customer service roles and within financial institutions. Automated decisioning will be responsible for tasks such as approving loans, deciding whether a customer should be onboarded or identifying corruption and financial crime.

Organisations will benefit from an increase in productivity as a result of greater automation, meaning more revenue will generated. This thus provides additional money to spend on supporting jobs in the services sector.Due to the vast array of jobs that could be impacted by AI, it is fundamental to address the potential pitfalls of these technologies. Business need to overcome the trust and bias issues surrounding AI by achieving an effective and successful implementation that makes it possible for everyone to benefit.

Governments must ensure that gains from AI are shared widely across society to prevent social inequality between those affected and unaffected by these developments. For example, this could be through increased investment into training. With the additional cost-savings from implementing AI systems, employers should also focus on upskilling their current employees.

To properly leverage the power of AI, we need to address the issue at an educational level, as well as in business. Education systems needs to focus on training students in roles directly associated to working with AI, including programmers and data analysts. This requires more emphasis to be put on STEM subjects (science, technology, engineering and mathematics). Also, subjects centered around building creative, social and emotional skills should be encouraged. Whilst artificial intelligence will be more productive than human workers for repetitive tasks, humans will always outperform machines in jobs requiring relationship-building and imagination. Hence, artificial intelligence will change our world both inside and outside the workplace. Instead of focusing on the fear surrounding automation, businesses need to embrace these new technologies to ensure they implement the most effective AI systems to enhance and compliment human intelligence.

Artificial Intelligence (AI) in Banking working environment

Artificial Intelligence (AI) is a fast-evolving technology, gaining popularity all around the world. Several industries have already adopted AI for various applications, getting better and smarter day by day. In the past few years, the banking sector has also become one of the leading adopters of Artificial Intelligence. Most banks and financial institutions are implementing AI to add more efficiency to their back-office and lessen security risks.

As per Statista, the AI market in the United States is forecasted to reach 7.35 billion U.S. dollars in 2018. Some major applications of AI include classification, image recognition, object identification, and automated geophysical feature detection. Speaking of banking and financial institutions, JPMorgan Chase, Wells Fargo, Bank of America, CitiBank, and other leading U.S. banks have already implemented AI in their systems, helping consumers manage their daily banking needs more efficiently.

AI technology can bring better Customer Support in bank service environment

Several pieces of evidence advocate that the customers willingly prefer self-service options which allow them to chat with a virtual assistant as if it were a live customer representative. Most leading banks have already added virtual assistants to their instant website chatbots, voice response systems, and mobile applications. Artificial Intelligence considers each interaction as a teachable moment, so the chatbots (virtual assistants) keeps getting better while understanding customers. With AI, virtual assistants can deliver better customer support. It also allows sentiment analysis, so the virtual assistant can determine when individuals are getting frustrated and instantly transfer them to a live agent.

Enhanced Banking Services

AI streamlines the banking process while giving customer service a new level of comfortability. It allows banks to meet customers' expectations with comprehensive digital support. With Artificial Intelligence, you can achieve greater precision and accuracy. From cash transfer to bills payment, cards management, and other support, AI can significantly enrich the satisfaction level of your customers. All of these operations can be easily managed through desktops, smartphones, and other mobile devices.

Scam Recognition

With an immense growth of banking fraud, scam recognition and reduction has become challenging for the banking sector. Several banks tried to identify the factors and powerful solutions but couldn't succeed. However, AI makes it easier to detect the factors involved in frauds and support investigators. It improves financial security with advanced fraud prevention tactics. Artificial Intelligence works as a real-time scam solution for the banking sector while handling complex situations and tactics. Based on advanced data crunching, AI can detect fraud by flagging unusual transactions. It also feeds back into the consumer's profile which subsequently builds a secure environment.

Advanced Data Analytics

One of the main advantages of AI is its ability to complete tedious tasks through intricate automation, resulting in better productivity. Based on a machine learning algorithm, AI can quickly consume and process a massive amount of data at an expedited level. The enormous speed brings efficiency to financial services, providing scope for personalized offerings to consumers. What's even more, AI makes faster decisions while carrying out actions quickly. With such advantages, it is nearly obvious that the majority of banks and financial institutions will adopt AI to stay competitive and deliver better customer support. However, several cons are also associated with a machine learning algorithm. As it continues to learn and grow, the decision-making capabilities may create problems in the near future.

Disadvanages of AI in Banking Sector

Artificial intelligence is also expected to massively disrupt banks and traditional financial services. Some of its disadvantages are listed below.

Highly Expensive

Production and maintenance of artificial intelligence demand huge costs since they are very complex machines. AI also consists of advanced software programs which require regular updates to meet the needs of the changing environment. In the case of critical failures, the procedure to reinstate the system and recover lost codes may require enormous time and cost.

Bad Calls

Though Artificial Intelligence can learn and improve, it still can't make judgment calls. Humans can take individual circumstances and judgment calls into account when making decisions, something that AI might never be able to do. Replacing adaptive human behavior with AI may cause irrational behavior within ecosystems of humans and things.

Distribution of Power

There is a constant fear of AI superseding or taking over the humans. Artificial intelligence can give a lot of power to the few individuals who are controlling it. Hence, AI carries the risk and takes control away from humans while dehumanizing actions in several ways.

Unemployment

Replacement of the workforce with machines can lead to wide-reaching unemployment. Moreover, if the use of AI becomes rampant, people will be highly dependent on the machines and lose their creative power. Unemployment is a socially undesirable issue. Individuals with nothing to do can lead to the devastating use of their minds. Be it banking or any other sector; Artificial intelligence can effectively increase the unemployment rate.

Artificial Intelligence delivered to wrong hands can turn out to be a serious threat to humankind. If individuals start thinking destructively, they can generate havoc with these advanced machines. The challenges introduced by the emergence of artificial intelligence revolve around several things. However, AI is a right balance of skill and emotions which is continually growing. Artificial intelligence provides banks, financial institutions, and tech companies with significant competitive advantages. Nevertheless, it can completely transform the financial sector and make it faster, but this will only be possible if the financial industry can manage the security risk of systems based on AI.

What does artificial intelligence mean for the bank service office workers?

With all these new artificial intelligence use cases comes the question of whether machines will force humans into obsolescence. The jury is still out: Some experts vehemently deny that artificial intelligence will automate so many jobs that millions of people find themselves unemployed, while other experts see it as a pressing problem.

"The structure of the workforce is changing, but I don't think artificial intelligence is essentially replacing jobs in bank service working environment. It allows us to really create a knowledge-based economy and leverage that to create better automation for a better form of life. It might be a little bit theoretical, but I think if you have to worry about artificial intelligence and robots replacing some bank service jobs, e.g. bank security, bank enquiry service,. But, AI can not replace bank counter service staffs to do saving or withdrawing money transfer tasks when any customers prepare to save money or withdraw money in bank counters. As this technology develops, the AI bank service will see new startups, numerous saving or withdraw transactions from consumer won't be raise more easily.

AI to Banking and Finance industry

The banking and finance industry plays a major role in our lives. I mean the world runs on money and banks are essentially the gatekeepers that regulate that flow. Did you know that the banking and finance industry heavily relies on artificial intelligence for things like customer service, fraud protection, investment, and more? A simple example is the automated emails that you receive from banks whenever you do an out of the ordinary transaction. Well, that's AI watching over your account and trying to warn you of any fraud.

AI is also being trained to look at large samples of fraud data and find a pattern so that you can be warned before it happens to you. Also, when you hitch a little snag and chat with bank's customer service, chances are that you are chatting with an AI bot. Even the big players in the finance industry use AI to analyze data to find the best avenues to invest money so they can get the most returns with the least risk. That's not all, AI is poised to play an even bigger role in the industry as major banks across the world are investing billions of dollars in the AI technology and we all will observe its effects sooner than later

How AI influences our daily working life in any office working environment

Can AI bring only disadvantages? If AI can bring disadvantges, what are its disadvantages to any working environment ?The entire tech world is debating the consequences of artificial intelligence and the part AI is going to play in shaping our future. While we might think that artificial intelligence is at least a few years away from causing any considerable effects on our lives, the fact remains that it is already having an enormous impact on us. Artificial intelligence is affecting our decisions and our lifestyles every day. Don't believe me? I shall indicate some product examples how AI anticipates which can influence our working culture in any office environment.

Examples of how Artificial Intelligence assistance to office working environment may include as below:

1. Smartphones

Smartphones have become the most indispensable tech product that we own today and we use it almost all the time. Well, if you are using a smartphone, you are interacting with AI whether you know it or not. From the obvious AI features such as the built-in smart assistants to not so obvious ones such as the portrait mode in the camera, AI is impacting our lives in every day office working environment.

In fact, the two examples that I provided that our working world of AI and how it is effecting our working lives. Firstly, there are the obvious AI elements which most of us have some knowledge about. For example, when you are using a smart assistant in office, whether it's Google Assistant, Alexa, Siri, or Bixby, you more or less know that these assistants are based on AI. However, when we are using a feature such as the portrait mode effect while shooting a picture, we never consider that AI might be behind that too. Have you ever thought how the Google Pixel phones or iPhones can capture such great portrait shots? The answer is artificial intelligence. So, when any office workers need to find any knowledge to solve their working problem immediately in any offices. They may apply AI smart phone tools to help them to apply online channel to search any new knowledge to attempt to solve their working problem in possible, when their computers have none any computers in offices.

Now more and more manufacturers are including AI in their smartphones with big chip manufacturers including Qualcomm and Huawei producing chips with built-in AI capabilities. The AI integration is helping in bringing features like scene detection, mixed and virtual reality elements, and more. AI is going to play an even major role in the coming years. We are already seeing the huge emphasis on AI with the latest Android and iOS updates. Features like app actions, splices, and adaptive battery in Android Pie and Siri shortcut and Siri suggestions in iOS 12 are made possible with AI. So, next time if any office workers think AI is not effecting them, take out your smartphone to replace computers to find any knowledge to help you to solve any tasks problems immediately in offices.

2. Social Media Feeds

If you are thinking that smart cars don't personally effect you as they are still not in your country or city, well, how about something which you use on a daily basis. Even if you are living under a rock, there's a high probability that you are tweeting from underneath it. If Twitter's not your choice of poison, maybe it's Facebook or Instagram, or Snapchat or any of the myriad of social media apps out there. Well, if you are using social media, most of your decisions are being impacted by artificial intelligence. So, any office workers may apply AI to help them to gather any new information to solve any difficult task problems , if their managers can not assist them to solve any sudden tasks problem, they are encountering to need to solve any working complex tasks problem internet social media in any any office working environment immediately.

From the feeds that office staffs can see in their working timeline to the notifications that you receive from these apps, everything is curated by AI. AI takes all your past behavior, web searches, interactions, and everything else that you do when you are on these websites and tailors the experience just for you. The sole purpose of AI here is to make the apps so addictive that you come back to them again and again, and I am ready to place a bet that AI is winning this war against you.

3. Online Ads Network

One of the biggest users of artificial intelligence is the online ad industry which uses AI to not only track user statistics but also serve us ads based on those statistics. Without AI, the online ad industry will just fail as it would show random ads to users with no connection to their preferences what so ever. AI has become so successful in determining our interests and serving us ads that the global digital ad industry has crossed 250 billion US dollars with the industry projected to cross the 300 billion mark in 2019. So next time when any product developers are going online and seeing ads or product recommendation, know that AI is impacting to any new products advertisement method more efficiently.

4. AI can be any office security

While we can all debate the ethics of using a broad surveillance system, there's no denying the fact that it is being used and AI is playing a big part in that. It is not possible for humans to keep monitoring multiple monitors with feeds from hundreds if not thousands of cameras at the same time, and hence, using AI makes perfect sense. With technologies like object recognition and facial recognition getting better and better every day, it won't be long when all the security camera feeds are being monitored by an AI and not a human. While there's still time before AI can be fully implemented such as security in any offices, this is going to be our future.

5. Smart Keyboard Apps

Smart Keyboard Apps. Granted, not everyone loves dealing with on-screen keyboards. However, they have become far more intuitive, allowing users to type comfortably and faster. What has probably proved to be a catalyst for them is the integration of AI. The smart keyboard apps keep a tab on the writing style of a user and predict words and emojis accordingly. Thus, typing on the touchscreen has become faster and more convenient. Not to mention, artificial intelligence also plays a vital role in pin-pointing misspellings and typos. So, any office workers can apply smart keyboard apps to help their to raise typing efficiency and reduce wrong typing word in error when they need to type any document in offices.

6. E-Commerce

` AI-driven algorithms have kind of given the much-needed impetus to e-commerce to provide a more personalized experience. According to several reports, its usage has vastly increased sales and also played a good part in building loyal relationships with customers. Thus, companies take advantage of AI to deploy chatbots to collect pivotal data and also predict purchases to create a customer-centric experience. Yet to come across this shift of strategy? Just spend some time with sites like Amazon and eBay and you will soon get to know how fast the landscape is changing around you – for the better! So, Ai can help any businesses to achieve e-commerce sale channel more easily.

7. Smart Email Apps

In any office working environment, if you still find your inbox cluttered with too many unwanted messages, chances are pretty high that you are still stuck with an old school email app. You heard it right! Modern email apps like Spark make the most of AI to get rid of spam messages and also categorize emails so that you can quickly access the important ones. What's more, they also offer smart replies based on the messages you receive to help you reply to any email quickly. The "Smart Reply" feature of Gmail is a great example of this. It uses AI to scan the text of the email and provides you with contextual answers. So, AI can help any office staffs to know who had sent any message from email and respond their email immediate , when AI can help any offices to avoid to receive any email spam rubbish email message in any time, even after working hours, it means that AI is working to help any office staffs to avoid to receive any email spam rubblish message in any time. So, when they go to office to work, even they go home after working hours. They can know whether what the important email messages are sent to their office email in boxes any time. Then, they can send email to respond their customers' enquires any time. So, AI can help any office workers can have chance to work at homes.

The Future of Artificial Intelligence In The Workplace

Smart technologies aren't just changing our homes; they're edging their way into their numerous industries and are disrupting the workplace. Artificial Intelligence (AI) has the potential to improve productivity, efficiency and accuracy across an organization – but is this entirely beneficial? Many fear that the rise of AI will lead to machines and robots replacing human workers and view this progression in technology as threat rather than a tool to better ourselves.

With AI continuing to be a prominent buzzword in 2019, businesses need to realize that self-learning and black-box capabilities are not the panacea. Many organisations are already beginning to see the incredible capabilities of AI, using these advantages to enhance human intelligence and gain real value from their data. As there is increasing evidence demonstrating the benefits of intelligent systems, more decision-makers in the boardroom are gaining a better understanding of what AI can really offer. Research conducted by EY explains "organizations enabling AI at the enterprise level are increasing operational efficiency, making faster, more informed decisions and innovating new products and services."

Today In: Cybersecurity

The first companies employing AI systems across the board will gain competitive advantage, reduce cost of operations and remove head counts. Whilst this may be a positive from a business perspective, it is obvious why this a worry for those working in roles at risk of displacement. The introduction of these technologies will likely trigger an issue with unions and job security due to the substantial operational changes. Although AI will affect every sector in some way, not every job is at equal risk. PwC predicts a relatively low displacement of jobs (around 3%) in the first wave of automation, but this could dramatically increase up to 30% by the mid-2030's. Occupations within the transport industry could potentially be at much greater risk, whereas jobs requiring social, emotional and literary abilities are at the lowest risk of displacement.

A positive future with artificial intelligence

Many businesses and individuals are optimistic that this AI-driven shift in the workplace will result in more jobs being created than lost. As we develop innovative technologies, AI will have a positive impact on our economy by creating jobs that require the skill set to implement new systems. 80% of respondents in the EY survey said it was the lack of these skills that was the biggest challenge when employing AI programs. It is likely that artificial intelligence will soon replace jobs involving repetitive or basic problem-solving tasks, and even go beyond current human capability. AI systems will be making decisions instead of humans in industrial settings, customer service roles and within financial institutions. Automated decisioning will be responsible for tasks such as approving loans, deciding whether a customer should be onboarded or identifying corruption and financial crime. Organisations will benefit from an increase in productivity as a result of greater automation, meaning more revenue will generated. This thus provides additional money to spend on supporting jobs in the services sector.

How to take advantage of AI to any offices

Due to the vast array of jobs that could be impacted by AI, it is fundamental to address the potential pitfalls of these technologies. Business need to overcome the trust and bias issues surrounding AI by achieving an effective and successful implementation that makes it possible for everyone to benefit. Governments must ensure that gains from AI are shared widely across society to prevent social inequality between those affected and unaffected by these developments. For example, this could be through increased investment into training.With the additional cost-savings from implementing AI systems, employers should also focus on upskilling their current employees.

To properly leverage the power of AI, we need to address the issue at an educational level, as well as in business. Education systems needs to focus on training students in roles directly associated to working with AI, including programmers and data analysts. This requires more emphasis to be put on STEM subjects (science, technology, engineering and mathematics). Also, subjects centered around building creative, social and emotional skills should be encouraged. Whilst artificial intelligence will be more productive than human workers for repetitive tasks, humans will always outperform machines in jobs requiring relationship-building and imagination. Artificial intelligence will change our world both inside and outside the workplace. Instead of focusing on the fear surrounding automation, businesses need to embrace these new technologies to ensure they implement the most effective AI systems to enhance and compliment human intelligence

How AI can help office workers to do tasks more easily

Companies are currently spending big on artificial intelligence and machine learning initiatives to the tune of $12 billion, but estimates put that figure as high as $57.6 billion by 2021, according to the International Data Corporation (IDC). With such massive shifts, the focus is usually on what we might lose, but it shouldn't be. A recent report on the future of work from the McKinsey Global Institute suggests that while only about 5% of jobs can be completely eliminated by automation, the rise of AI requires workers to beef up both technical and soft skills in order to stay competitive.

What's seldom discussed is how AI can revolutionize our jobs. It's now possible to pinpoint peak productivity for a single day, improve communication in meetings (even before people ever work together face to face), or even teach you to be a better leader, all thanks to AI platforms. I shall indicate these advantages to bring any office benefits from AI assistance as below:

1. AI can help any companies to get better to hire the best applicants

AI has the greatest potential to change the way companies find candidates, according to Alexander Rinke, cofounder and CEO of Celonis. The company's process-mining technology helps businesses to understand the areas where automation can help humans, he says. In HR departments, Celonis can help identify how fast workers come and go, the cost per hire, and which positions take the longest to fill. AI helped enable one customer's ability to identify bottlenecks in recruitment and reduced process costs internally by 30% as well as get them hired more quickly, he says.

Crafting a resume has never been easier, nor has landing an interview.

Another example is how recruitment software provider iCIMS, in partnership with Google, is helping job seekers find jobs directly through the search engine, thanks to Google's AI and machine learning capabilities. Susan Vitale, iCIMS's chief marketing officer says that in addition to reducing the number of expired job postings, machine learning is underlying a private beta program of Google's Cloud Jobs Discovery model. "For a candidate searching for, say, a CTO role, Cloud Job Discovery will serve up CTO positions as well as jobs with titles that are similar, but not verbatim, such as chief technology officer or chief technical officer," says Vitale. This model also allows for conceptual search results, such as serving up job listings for cashiers, sales associates, and store associates when someone searches for one versus just only showing jobs that exactly match the keyword search criteria, she adds.

2. AI can help any office workers to raise much more productive efficiencies

John Furneaux, CEO and cofounder of Hive, says predictive analytics will help us better understand how we work. "It can tell us just about everything we want to know about teams and collaboration, for example, if men or women get more done in the afternoon, and if summer Fridays are a myth," he says. (Everyone thinks summer Fridays aren't productive, but in reality there's no difference between those and other Fridays during the year–productivity is equally low.)

Using a data set of over 30,000 completed actions across Hive workspaces, Furneaux says they were able to identify some notable trends in productivity. For example, men were far more productive early in the day, with a sharp decline in the afternoon, while women had a slower start to the day but were far more productive in later hours than their male counterparts. And analyzing chat messages revealed that women appear to complete more tasks when chatting, suggesting they use communication as a key tool to completing work. Similarly, Nintex Hawkeye analyzes data on business processes by types, users, roles, and departments to see who's doing the work and how long it takes them to do it. Management can monitor and analyze those metrics in real time.

3. AI can help any managers to make the most fair compensation and eliminate wage gaps to every staffs

Tanya Jansen, cofounder of the compensation management platform beqom, says that AI and predictive analytics can eliminate unconscious bias from compensation. Jansen says that AI based on a variety of rules including education, experience, certifications, and more can make compensation more fair and help businesses move closer to closing pay gaps. "Specifically, AI can help solve gender pay gaps and the CEO-to-worker pay gap, in which pay ratios of Fortune 500 companies range from 2:1 at the low end to nearly 5000:1 at the high end," she says. Additionally, the use of AI-driven compensation technology to make pay more fair can mitigate the risk of employee turnover, which costs businesses as much as 33% of a worker's annual salary to replace them.

4. AI can help any office staffs to arrange better meetings
Augmented Reality (AR) is still in its infancy, but AI and machine learning are the core components that make it work. As such, Christa Manning, the vice president and solution provider research leader at Bersin, Deloitte Consulting LLP, says that AR can help workers find the right information, in the right place, at the right time to make the best decisions wherever they may be working. For example, as more companies adopt video meetings and collaborative workspaces, it's likely we'll begin to see HR-curated information like talent profiles and work styles layered over interactions through AR."Imagine being in a video conference with a colleague and having direct insight into their communication style, seeing tips on how to best interact with them or reminders of what needs to be discussed. SO, AI can help any organizations to conclude or find the best methods to solve any problems after their every discussion in any meetings.
How AI is improving onboarding and training. AI coaching tools first learn by observing how different employees conduct specific tasks. Then these tools can walk new employees through how to complete those tasks—or even coach existing employees on how to do things more effectively or efficiently. Chorus is a great example of this technology. It analyzes sales calls while they happen, offering tips to help sales reps manage the cadence of meetings and use the most effective messaging. It also records all sales calls and compiles statistics for each sales rep, providing everyone with the tools they need to help them close more deals and conduct more effective calls. Another example is Cogito, a tool that combines AI with behavioral science to help customer service employees provide better phone support. It monitors calls for voice signals, providing real-time suggestions to representatives on how to improve the conversation.

5. AI can help any managers to be better leaders
Indiggo, a platform powered by a proprietary AI tool called "indi," functions as a brain that has consumed all the knowledge the company has gathered

in its 15 years of operation. It also uses an algorithm to provide an estimate of how much time is wasted by a company by analyzing the size of its management team. Then it taps their calendars to see how they spend their time, and walks individual managers through a type of Q&A to make sure they are clear on what their top three priorities are, and how that relates to the organization's priorities, which will indicate if that strategy is moving forward or not. "The counterintuitive impact of these advances is that they actually make human work truly irreplaceable," Alexander Rinke, the cofounder and CEO of Celonis says. As such, he reminds us, "Humans are much better at processes that involve reasoning, judgment, and interaction with people." So, AI can recommend more accurate and useful opinions to help any managers to solve their managing challenges in office any time.

How AI is eliminating repetitive administrative tasks
There are a lot of tasks that knowledge workers spend time on that provide little—if any—value.For example, say you need to schedule a meeting to get consensus on a decision before moving forward, but you need five people to join the meeting. It's easy to spend a ton of time sending email back-and-forth or finding an open slot on everyone's calendar.That's not the most rewarding use of your time for you or your company.Tools like X.ai give employees AI-powered personal assistants that perform administrative tasks like scheduling, rescheduling, and cancelling meetings.

How AI is transforming internal communications and support
Personnel on the teams that provide employee support have their hands full with other responsibilities, too. HR teams work on building the kind of company people love working for. IT maintains the company's network and keeps data secure. Office managers frequently run big events like holiday parties.These tasks are crucial, but they're often hard for teams to focus on because they're busy answering routine questions. AI service desks like askSpoke allow employee support teams to balance their service commitments with other important responsibilities by reducing interruptions from rote, repetitive requests.Employees can askSpoke for whatever they need over Slack, email, SMS, and the web. askSpoke's friendly AI will automatically provide a prompt response.

How AI is transforming marketing, sales, and customer service
AI-powered chatbots help with external support as well. Just like with internal support tools like askSpoke, these chatbots learn from real marketers, salespeople, and customer service reps and are eventually able to answer questions as accurately as a knowledgeable person.For example,

chatbot for Messenger helps customers plan their vacations. It books flights, hotels, and cars, highlights destination attractions, and even provides answers to questions like "Where can I go for $100 expense budget only?"

How AI is transforming business data and analytics

It's hard to run a competitive business today without data. But even massive amounts of data are useless without a way to transform that data into valuable insights. That's typically why you'd want to hire a data scientist—which just happens to be one of the most difficult roles to fill. How AI is fighting fraud and transforming security. Have you ever taken a call from your bank to find that someone used your debit card fraudulently? Most likely, your bank used some form of AI to detect the fraudulent transaction and decline it. Applying the same basic technology to the workplace helps identify security risks and keeps customer, employee, and company data safe. AI-powered software can automatically detect and address threats among thousands or millions of signals that humans would never be able to parse (especially not in real-time).

How AI is transforming productivity

While AI is transforming the workplace in many different ways across every industry, it's impacting productivity most of all. When your office staffs don't have to scroll through calendars to look for open meeting times, build reports in spreadsheets to look for insights, or spend your day answering the same questions over and over again, you're more productive. Workers are freed from redundant and mindless tasks, giving them more time to do work that matters, solve problems, and exercise their creativity. Some tools use AI to specifically monitor and boost productivity. For example, Deloitte's LaborWise provides company leaders and managers with productivity analytics that help them identify areas where labor costs are too high, impediments that slow people down, and departments that need additional staff.

In conclusion, what AI means for the workplace of the future. While some will dramatize the negative impacts of AI, cognitive computing, and robotics, these powerful tools will also help create new jobs, boost productivity, and allow workers to focus on the human aspects of work. Essentially, automation frees companies and their employees up to be more empathetic, to focus on things like the customer experience, employee engagement, and workplace culture.

What are traditional office tools to be replaced by AI ?

Artificial intelligence (AI) is predicted to eliminate over a million jobs in the next few years, potentially replacing lower level positions like administrative assistants with humanoid robots or voice assistants. But in the nearer future, fresh AI-driven software and products are also moving to eliminate non-human elements of the workplace by replacing traditional office tools, including both physical products and everyday electronic processes. Why should businesses switch from the tried-and-true to emerging technology? Many of the experts TechRepublic talked to said the AI options streamline business practices, making their adopters work smarter instead of harder. I shall indicate these office tools ,they can be applied to help any office staffs to finish their these tasks in office, they may include as below:

1. Scheduling

Workloud's end-to-end, cloud-based workforce management software takes scheduling from paper or Excel and moves it to the cloud. Everything from clocking in and out to monitoring employee absences is fully digitalized.Schedules and timesheets are accurate, created easily, and accessible through the service's web, tablet, and mobile apps. The software can also be used for absence management.

2. Employee talent selection

Using AI and organizational behavior science, can be used to replace internal spreadsheets and databases designed to monitor human capital. By mining employee attributes and experiences, the software can recommend who would be best for a project. The software also collects reviews after projects to better predict successful employee-project matches.The traditional hiring process is slow, biased and inaccurate, By removing humans from the beginning stages of the process, it can become faster and more fair, and result in better hires.

AI software automates the hiring process, using online simulations instead of manual screenings and interviews. Using the software, employers can include tasks in a job application, allowing job candidates to show technical skills that may be necessary for a job. Employers can't rule out candidates until they see how the candidate performs, eliminating bias that occurs in the resume reading stage. Both sides also automatically receive updates about each other's steps, reducing the amount of time it takes to .

3.Timesheets: Allocate

Using AI and machine learning, the software registers an employee's computer activity throughout the day. The data, which can also pull information from email and calendars, is used to suggest timesheet entries to reflect a more accurate amount of time an employee spent working. The employee can review and revise as necessary. However, the software doesn't spy on or monitor employees. The data is only available to each employee, while others in the company can only see the timesheet's output, which Allocate said would be the same information available if a manual sheet was used. So,replacing manual timesheets with Allocate has three advantages: More accurate time entry, project analytics, and "'unsucking' the work experience."

4. Document storage

By using AI to read and analyze business and legal documents, AI can store all of the important document-based information in the cloud. The severe reduction in print-outs means less paper and ink, fewer products like binder clips and boxes to store and organize all of the paper, and more employee time freed up from not needing to manually sort through every document.

For example, in any lawyer offices, legal professionals' morale in the industry can suffer when they are pushed into performing such dull, repetitive tasks like sorting through and coding documents by hand, With AI tools to automate those duties, lawyers can focus on more meaningful projects and boost the business's and clients' success as a result. While focused on law firms, businesses that have a lot of unstructured data in documents may also be able to use the service to free up employee time and save on printing costs.

5. Scanners: Adobe Scan

While documents are moving to the cloud more and more, sometimes a physical copy of a document still needs to be scanned using a bulky office scanner. Adobe Scan, an app that condenses a scanner to the size of a smartphone, can rid offices of the need for an in-house scanner. Users can download and open the app, then hold their device over whatever they need to scan. Adobe Sensei then turns the scan into a PDF, and sends it to the Adobe Document Cloud. The app can transform any image into digital text that can then be searched and used electronically. The app streamlines the scanning process, making scans cleaner and more immediate. For businesses already using Adobe services, the app makes documents easily accessible.

6. Landline phones

While landlines in homes are increasingly less common, the same cannot be said for offices. But using chatbots and AI integrations, RingCentral is trying to replace traditional office landline phone systems. The platform offers over 100 integrations, including that AI landline phones can let employees check their voicemail, and a Gong.io option that listens to call recordings to find traits of successful employees than can be used in training. An add-on for Gmail lets users switch from emailing back and forth to a voice session without needing to look up contact information. AI landline phone is easy to adopt and use in the workplace, and is more customizable than standard phone systems, said David Lee, vice president of platform products. Compared to the traditional option, the cloud-based option is "future-proof.

How artificial intelligence can raise office efficiency

Artificial Intelligence is already impacting every industry through automation and machine learning, bringing concerns that AI is on the fast track to replacing many jobs. But these fears aren't new, says Dan Jackson, director of Enterprise Technology at Crestron, a company that designs workplace technology. "I'd argue this is no different than when we moved from an agricultural to an industrial economy at the turn of the last century. The percentage of people working in agriculture significantly decreased, and it was a big shift, but we still have plenty of jobs 100 years later," he says. Anytime society experiences a major technological advancement, we need to be prepared for it to change the way we live and work. It's hard to imagine what the future of jobs will look like with AI, but that future exists. And optimists suggest that, like the sewing machine to the textile industry, AI will make us better, more efficient and faster workers.

In fact, many experts agree that AI has the potential to eliminate mundane, administrative work, while we will always rely on human workers to be empathetic, collaborative, creative and strategic. But it's impact on any industry lies in the hands of the business leaders who are responsible for adopting AI strategies.

● Training presents challenges

A recent study of 1,000 global companies by Accenture found that AI is already creating three new categories of jobs: trainers, explainers and sustainers. Trainers are the people who teach AI systems how to act -- whether it's language, human behavior or the intricacies of human interaction. Explainers are the liaison between technology and business leaders, providing more insight and clarity into machine learning for the non-tech workers. Sustainers are the workers required to maintain AI systems and troubleshoot any potential issues. Some jobs were highly technical and required advanced degrees, but other roles demanded innately human things such as empathy and interaction. Downstream jobs, such as those in sales, marketing, or service will change to take advantage of the insights from AI, but many of the core skills will remain. However, it might sound like any job related to AI will require years of technical knowledge, but that isn't the case. We've already seen a shift in tech hiring -- companies often need highly specific skill sets that are hard to find in potential candidates. As a result, more businesses are hiring employees with the right soft skills, and then training them in technical skills.

An office effort measured approach to AI

The real takeaway is that any approach to AI will need to consider the human aspect of every business. AI has great potential to increase efficiency and accuracy and it's already been proven in certain industries. For example, the use of AI In banking to identify and money laundering schemes. It's also improved healthcare by "increasing the speed and accuracy" of cancer diagnosistics. AI can also help reduce the cost and length of human trafficking investigations, a situation where time is precious. In these examples, AI hasn't replaced jobs, but has positively impacted efficiency.

Thus, we need to ensure our education system responds to equip young people with the appropriate skills and adaptability, while businesses and public organizations must invest in training. Perhaps most of all, we need to encourage imagination and willingness to experiment. The organizations that can innovate with AI will reap the benefits. Their growth will make them the primary source of future jobs. Companies have a choice when implementing AI. They can choose to effectively implement systems that make employee's lives easier and find creative ways to leverage the technology. It's up to employers to ease fears for workers around AI and build strategies that benefit everyone. Hence, some AI experts believe AI can only raise efficiency to some office tasks, however, AI can not still raise efficiency to all office tasks for any office deparments. The reasons are because some office tasks which can only dominate to finish by human office workers. These office tasks are as below:

How can leaders and managers improve employee productivity while still saving time? These below tasks, AI experts ensure that AI can not help any office workers to raise their efficiencies as below:

1. Office managers can not delegate to AI to help them to do. While this tip might seem the most obvious, it is often the most difficult to put into practice. We get it–your company is your baby, so you want to have a direct hand in everything that goes on with it. While there is nothing

wrong with prioritizing quality (it is what makes a business successful, after all), checking over every small detail yourself rather than delegating can waste everyone's valuable time. Instead, give responsibilities to qualified employees, and trust that they will perform the tasks well. This gives your employees the opportunity to gain skills and leadership experience that will ultimately benefit your company. You hired them for a reason, now give them a chance to prove you right.

2. Office managers can not match Tasks to Skills to AI. Knowing your employees' skills and behavioral styles is essential for maximizing efficiency. For example, an extroverted, creative, out-of-the-box thinker is probably a great person to pitch ideas to clients. However, they might struggle if they are given a more rule-intensive, detail-oriented task. Asking your employees to be great at everything just isn't efficient–instead, before giving an employee an assignment, ask yourself: is this the person best suited to perform this task? If not, find someone else whose skills and styles match your needs.

3. Office managers can not teach AI to replace them how to communicate and teach their low level staffs how to work effectively. Every manager knows that communication is the key to a productive workforce. Technology has allowed us to contact each other with the mere click of a button (or should we say, tap of a touch screen)–this naturally means that current communication methods are as efficient as possible, right? Not necessarily. A McKinsey study found that emails can take up nearly 28% of an employee's time. In fact, email was revealed to be the second most time-consuming activity for workers (after their job-specific tasks). Instead of relying solely on email, try social networking tools (such as Slack) designed for even quicker team communication. You can also encourage your employees to occasionally adopt a more antiquated form of contact...voice-to-voice communication. Having a quick meeting or phone call can settle a matter that might have taken hours of back-and-forth emails. All of above communication tasks, I believe that AI can not do better than managers in offices.

4. AI can not keep Goals Clear and focused to be better than managers. You can't expect employees to be efficient if they don't have a focused goal to aim for. If a goal is not clearly defined and actually achievable, employees will be less productive. So, try to make sure employees' assignments are as clear and narrow as possible. Let them know exactly what you expect of them, and tell them specifically what impact this assignment will have.

One way to do this is to make sure your goals are "SMART" – specific, measurable, attainable, realistic, and timely. Before assigning an employee a task, ask yourself if it fits each of these requirements. If not, ask yourself how the task can be tweaked to help your workers stay focused and efficient.

5. AI can not know how to incentivize Employees to work more efficiently. One of the best ways to encourage employees to be more efficient is to actually give them a reason to do so. Recognizing your workers for a job well done will make them feel appreciated and encourage them to continue increasing their productivity. When deciding how to reward efficient employees, make sure you take into account their individual needs or preferences. For example, one employee might appreciate public recognition, while another would prefer a private "thank you." In addition to simple words of gratitude, here are a few incentives managers can know how to incentivize their staffs to work efficiently, but AI is only one machine, it can not perform very good.

6. AI does not know how to assist managers to train and Develop employees. Reducing training, or cutting it all together, might seem like a good way to save company time and money (learning on the job is said to be an effective way to train, after all). However, this could ultimately backfire. Forcing employees to learn their jobs on the fly can be extremely inefficient.
So, instead of having workers haphazardly trying to accomplish a task with zero guidance, take the extra day to teach them the necessary skills to do their job. This way, they can set about accomplishing their tasks on their own, and your time won't be wasted down the road answering simple questions or correcting errors. Past their original training, encourage continued employee development. Helping them expand their skillsets will build a much more advanced workforce, which will benefit your company in the long run. There are a number of ways you can support employee development: individual coaching, workshops, courses, seminars, shadowing or mentoring, or even just increasing their responsibilities. Offering these opportunities will give employees additional skills that allow them to improve their efficiency and productivity. But, AI do not know how to improve any office workers' performance more easily than managers.
● How can AI be dangerous to office working environment?

Most researchers agree that a superintelligent AI is unlikely to exhibit human emotions like love or hate, and that there is no reason to expect AI to become intentionally benevolent or malevolent. Instead, when considering how AI might become a risk to any office working environments, experts think two scenarios most likely:

The AI is programmed to do something devastating: Autonomous weapons are artificial intelligence systems that are programmed to kill. In the hands of the wrong person, these weapons could easily cause mass casualties. Moreover, an AI arms race could inadvertently lead to an AI war that also results in mass casualties. To avoid being thwarted by the enemy, these weapons would be designed to be extremely difficult to simply "turn off," so humans could plausibly lose control of such a situation. This risk is one that's present even with narrow AI, but grows as levels of AI intelligence and autonomy increase. So, if some businessmen apply AI to be business weapon to attack or steal their business competitors' business secret, e.g. contract document, employee performance report, profit report, even business secret document. Then, AI will be one business competitor weapon more than business assistant role in any business market. So, whether AI is office assistant or business competitor weapon, it depends on how the businessmen apply them to assist their business development.

The AI is programmed to do something beneficial, but it develops a destructive method for achieving its goal: This can happen whenever we fail to fully align the AI's goals with ours, which is strikingly difficult. If you ask an obedient intelligent car to take you to the airport as fast as possible, it might get you there chased by helicopters and covered in vomit, doing not what you wanted but literally what you asked for. If a superintelligent system is tasked with a ambitious geoengineering project, it might wreak havoc with our ecosystem as a side effect, and view human attempts to stop it as a threat to be met.

As these examples illustrate, the concern about advanced AI isn't malevolence but competence. A super-intelligent AI will be extremely good at accomplishing its goals, and if those goals aren't aligned with ours, we have a problem. You're probably not an evil ant-hater who steps on ants out of malice, but if you're in charge of a hydroelectric green energy project and there's an anthill in the region to be flooded, too bad for the ants. A key goal of AI safety research is to never place humanity in the position of those ants. Because AI has the potential to become more intelligent than any human, we have no surefire way of predicting how it will behave. We can't use past technological developments as much of a basis because we've never created anything that has the ability to, wittingly or unwittingly, outsmart us. The best example of what we could face may be our own evolution. People now control the planet, not because we're the strongest, fastest or biggest, but because we're the smartest. If we're no longer the smartest, are we assured to remain in control?

A captivating conversation is taking place about the future of artificial intelligence and what it will/should mean for humanity. There are fascinating controversies where the world's leading experts disagree, such as: AI's future impact on the job market; if/when human-level AI will be developed; whether this will lead to an intelligence explosion; and whether this is something we should welcome or fear. But there are also many examples of of boring pseudo-controversies caused by people misunderstanding and talking past each other. To help ourselves focus on the interesting controversies and open questions — and not on the misunderstandings — let's clear up some of the most common myths.

There have been a number of surveys asking AI researchers how many years from now they think we'll have human-level AI with at least 50% probability. All these surveys have the same conclusion: the world's leading experts disagree, so we simply don't know. For example, in such a poll of the AI researchers at the 2015 Puerto Rico AI conference, the average (median) answer was by year 2045, but some researchers guessed hundreds of years or more. There's also a related myth that people who worry about AI think it's only a few years away. In fact, most people on record worrying about superhuman AI guess it's still at least decades away. But they argue that as long as we're not 100% sure that it won't happen this century, it's smart to start safety research now to prepare for the eventuality. Many of the safety problems associated with human-level AI are so hard that they may take decades to solve. So, any businessmen ought have business moralty to know whether they ought how to apply their AI to assist their business development in our future office environment to be more moral.

● Five ways to use AI to improve business efficiency to these office tasks

Regardless of a company's size or type, its executives typically look for ways to help it operate as efficiently as possible. They understand the link between efficiency and profitability. If employees waste too much time with drawn-out processes or complicated tasks, it'll be hard for the enterprise to remain profitable and adapt to challenges. Fortunately, artificial intelligence

(AI) supports the need for effective business operations. Here are five ways enterprises can use AI for help: 5 ways to use AI to improve business efficiency image.Getting the best results from AI means looking at where bottlenecks exist, then figuring out if and how it might remove or minimise them. AI can help any offices to improve or raise efficiency to these tasks aspects as below:

1. Use AI to answer queries and support customer engagement

Chatbots are an increasingly popular option for businesses to try, and they use AI to work. Companies often build chatbots that can answer any questions from customers that come through outside of business hours. Some identify the nature of a person's problem, then either attempt to tackle it with preprogrammed answers or pass the communications to a human support worker. The retail industry, in particular, saw success by deploying chatbots. Global data collected by Juniper Research shows an estimated 2.6 billion retail-based chatbot interactions in 2019, and the company forecasts the number to rise to 22 billion in 2023.

Chatbots are excellent for answering simple questions like "How late are you open today?" or "Do you have gluten-free menu options?" Getting quick answers to queries like those increases the chances customers will choose to do business with one company over another. Equally importantly, when chatbots can give responses in a matter of seconds, there's no need for humans to stop what they're doing and address the questions.

2. To enhance reporting speed and accuracy

Company reports reveal things such as which products are selling the fastest and where they're most popular. They can also confirm the impacts of marketing campaigns on product sales, break down the costs of a new packaging choice or shipping method, and much more. However, as anyone that files reports knows, creating them is a painstaking task, and trying to rush through the process could cause mistakes. Some forward-thinking companies are combining AI with big data analytics. Doing this brings better forecasts and takes some of the burdens off the people who prepare the reports. AI also helps conquer the inevitability of mistakes. Even the most careful people make blunders, often because of mental fatigue.

AI learns to spot patterns in data and gets smarter with time. This means reports get finished faster and contain more-reliable information. The reliability aspect is crucial, especially since recently published research indicated two-thirds of the senior executives polled had no confidence or trust in big data. Using AI does not mean companies can do without data scientists. However, depending on the technology allows them to reduce the uncertainty that may otherwise exist. It also prevents employees who work with a company's data from being asked to recheck the findings, even if they initially took appropriate precautions to ensure accuracy.

    3. To improve data transfer speeds

Fast data transfers help AI technology work. Concerning some information-intensive applications like virtual reality (VR), any slow transmissions greatly interfere with the realism, and content immersion people should enjoy after strapping on a VR headset. As it turns out, AI can improve data transfer speeds, too. For example, services exist that boost speeds across any wide-area network (WAN). Users enjoy consistently accelerated rates regardless of the kind of information transferred. Some companies have solutions that can reduce WAN job times by up to 98%. These AI-driven options work particularly well when companies need to move information between data centres or cloud environments.

    4. To assist the IT team with identifying genuine cyberthreats and anomalies

One of the ongoing challenges faced by IT teams of all sizes is to separate the true cyber threats from false alarms. The difficulties associated with categorising the two types may mean cybersecurity professionals waste time getting to the bottom of things that are ultimately nonissues. They might miss the actual threats that could derail a company's operations. Besides detecting possible intrusions associated with a network, AI can screen for software abnormalities that may make it easier for cybercriminals to orchestrate their attacks successfully. It can also find malicious software hackers installed. Due to this kind of information and the advantages of receiving it through real-time updates, IT security teams can work more productively. They can use the majority of their resources on the threats that matter most to the company's stability.

Some organisations have even used AI to help them conquer the substantial skills shortage in the cybersecurity industry. At Texas A&M University, the Security Operations Center deals with about a million attempted hacks each month. The facility has some full-time workers, but students comprise most of the staff. They work alongside AI that aids in threat monitoring, detection and remediation. Before students see possible threats, the smart technology finds and groups them. This approach saves time and lets the team get to work investigating the problems and deciding how to handle them.

5. To streamline the time-to-hire metric when filling new positions
Statistics show the average time required to hire a person for an open position ranges from 12.7 to 49 days, depending on the industry. The timing also varies based on the type of work a job requires. For example, it takes a shorter amount of time overall to find someone for an administrative or human resources position than one associated with a creative or advertising role. Then, of course, interviews are more extensive for high-profile work. Human resources professionals increasingly use AI to cut down on the time between first posting a job and finding the ideal individual to hire. For example, an AI platform could look for particular desired keywords in submitted resumes, saving hiring managers from poring over the documents themselves. AI can also pitch in during interviews. A company called VCV recently raised $1.7m to further develop its AI tool that has voice and facial recognition components. Candidates are asked to record videos of them answering interview questions, but they can't prepare for the specific content in advance.

In conclusion, AI Can Boost Efficiency at All Types of Companies. The examples here highlight why so many company leaders conclude that if they use AI, they could cut down on inefficiencies. Getting the best results from AI means looking at where bottlenecks exist, then figuring out if and how it might remove or minimise them. But, AI still lack enough effort to help all staffs to raise efficiency to all department tasks in any office environments.

● How the office energy Department is using AI to solve some of their office staffs electricity toughest challenges in their office working environment.

Insights from artifical intelligence has the potential to transform nearly every aspect of the world as we know it. Today, it is being applied to accelerate the pace of discovery in a wide variety of areas including energy, materials science, health care, national security, emergency response, transportation, and more. AI can be trained to help any energy department to gather data to avoid energy waste to be used to any organizations. So, AI is such as one super machine to do more accurate judgement to help any energy scientists to find the best methods to help any organizations to avoid to waste to use any energy daily. Then, organizations can avoid to spend too much energy to use in offices and they can save more money and avoid energy shortage challenge causes more easily. When the office managers can apply AI ability to reason and put it into a more automated format in a computer system to their every staffs' computer and record their computer electricity use record in their offices every day.

How can AI help offices to save energy or avoid to waste energy ?

The next industrial revolution is already happening. Artificial intelligence (AI) is ushering in an era of technologies that are faster, more adaptable, more efficient, and making the world more digitally connected. AI is best described as complementary to human intelligence, delivering the computing power to crunch numbers too big for people and recognize patterns too tedious for the human eye. In a Harvard Business Review study of 1,500 companies, it was found that the most significant performance improvements were made when humans and machines worked together. As AI becomes one of society's greatest assets, it's especially helpful for solving problems that seem larger than life — like protecting our natural environment.

Through machine learning, robotics, drones, and the internet of things (IoT), society can achieve better monitoring, understanding, and prevention of damage and stressors on Earth's land, air, and water. Even technology already available today could reduce energy usage in the U.S. by 12 to 22 percent, according to The Information Technology Industry Council (ITI). In the face of this dire reality, the potential of technology to help meet this challenge is a rare source of optimism. According to a recent survey by Intel and the research firm Concentrix, 74 percent of business-decision makers working in environmental sustainability agree artificial intelligence (AI) will help solve long-standing environmental challenges; 64 percent agree the Internet of Things (IoT) will help solve these challenges. As the field of AI develops, so will the potential to protect the environment. From the land and air to both drinking and ocean water, AI is shaping up to be the key that governments, organizations, and individuals can tap to work toward a cleaner planet, even AI can help offices to avoid to waste energy when staffs are working in offices every day.

Many AI scientists indicate that AI will also make renewable energy technology like solar panels and wind turbines more efficient and cost effective, helping them to become ubiquitous and lower society's dependence on fossil fuels. AI will also make renewable energy technology like solar panels and wind turbines more efficient and cost effective, helping them to become ubiquitous and lower society's dependence on the fossil fuels polluting the air — then hopefully eliminate them all together. Combined with the smart grid, another technology that will be enabled by AI, this will truly progress the way people receive and use electricity in their homes, offices, and everywhere else. Smart meters save energy by allowing for two-way communication between the grid and anything that uses electricity, giving energy providers a better understanding of usage and the ability to make real-time adjustments for efficiency. Customers will benefit from the real-time data too; seeing the increased costs at peak times will encourage them to voluntarily adjust their usage to save money. This will, in turn, save even more energy: a win-win. Plus, the process of delivering the energy itself will also be improved by the smart grid, thanks to Volt/VAR control systems that can reduce the amount of energy wasted when it's in electricity transmission lines.

Can AI replace office workers

Can AI replace all office workers to do their different tasks in office different department ? If AI can only replace some department office workers to do their simple tasks, how it can raise more efficiency to compare them in some business office environments. I shall indicate some office tasks to explain how AI can help these businesses to raise their efficiency in officesas below:

● AI insurance workers

Nowadays, some country offices begin apply robotics to replace human office workers in their companies. For example, Japanese company replaces office workers with artificial intelligence in insurance industry. A future in which human workers are replaced by machines is about to become a reality at an insurance firm in Japan, where more than 30 employees are being laid off and replaced with an artificial intelligence system that can calculate payouts to policyholders.

Fukoku Mutual Life Insurance believes it will increase productivity by 30% and see a return on its investment in less than two years. The firm said it would save about 140m yen (£1m) a year after the 200m yen (£1.4m) AI system is installed this month. Maintaining it will cost about 15m yen (£100k) a year. The move is unlikely to be welcomed, however, by 34 employees who will be made redundant by the end of March.

The system is based on IBM's Watson Explorer, which, according to the tech firm, possesses "cognitive technology that can think like a human", enabling it to "analyse and interpret all of your data, including unstructured text, images, audio and video".The technology will be able to read tens of thousands of medical certificates and factor in the length of hospital stays, medical histories and any surgical procedures before calculating payouts, according to the Mainichi Shimbun.

While the use of AI will drastically reduce the time needed to calculate Fukoku Mutual's payouts – which reportedly totalled 132,000 during the current financial year – the sums will not be paid until they have been approved by a member of staff, the newspaper said.

Japan's shrinking, ageing population, coupled with its prowess in robot technology, makes it a prime testing ground for AI. According to a 2015 report by the Nomura Research Institute, nearly half of all jobs in Japan could be performed by robots by 2035. For example, one Japan insurance company, Dai-Ichi Life Insurance has already introduced a Watson-based system to assess payments - although it has not cut staff numbers - and Japan Post Insurance is interested in introducing a similar setup, the Mainichi said. AI could soon be playing a role in the country's politics. Next month, the economy, trade and industry ministry will introduce AI on a trial basis to help civil servants draft answers for ministers during cabinet meetings and parliamentary sessions. The ministry hopes AI will help reduce the punishingly long hours bureaucrats spend preparing written answers for ministers.

● AI public service workers

The automated city: do we still need humans to run public services? If the experiment is a success, it could be adopted by other government agencies, according the Jiji news agency. If, for example a question is asked about energy-saving policies, the AI system will provide civil servants with the relevant data and a list of pertinent debating points based on past answers to similar questions.

The march of Japan's AI robots hasn't been entirely glitch-free, however. At the end of last year a team of researchers abandoned an attempt to develop a robot intelligent enough to pass the entrance exam for the prestigious Tokyo University. "AI is not good at answering the type of questions that require an ability to grasp meanings across a broad spectrum," Noriko Arai, a professor at the National Institute of Informatics, told Kyodo news agency. Hence, AI will have possible to replace some public service workers' tasks.

● AI replace warehouse workers

Denso's use of Drishti shows how some jobs will be transformed by artificial intelligence even when they're unlikely to be eliminated by AI anytime soon. Many jobs in manufacturing require dexterity and resourcefulness, for example, in ways that robots and software still can't match. But advances in AI and sensors are providing new ways to digitize manual labor. That gives managers new insights—and potentially leverage—on workers. For example,some workers say the results are unpleasant. Last year, Amazon warehouse employees in Minnesota staged a walkout to protest how the company uses inventory and worker-tracking technology. They allege that Amazon uses it to enforce a punishing working pace that causes injuries. The company has disputed those claims, saying it coaches employees on how to safely meet quotas.

Workers at Denso were initially wary of the prospect of being video-recorded all day to feed machine-learning algorithms, but Huffman says they have since come to appreciate Drishti's technology. After something goes wrong, workers can now look at the data and video with their managers, instead of having to hope bosses take their account of what happened seriously. Huffman says having a constant readout on productivity also helps managers be more responsive to nascent problems. "If somebody's struggling, not every associate is going to call for help," he says. "If we see their cycle time is jumping through the roof, we can go over and say 'Are you having any issues?'"Workers on Denso lines equipped with Drishti's technology now get a personal feed of their own data. Monitors on each workstation display how a worker is doing, says Raja Shembekar, a Denso vice president. If the worker completes their assembly step on time, they see a smiley face—if not, a frowny one. Hence, Amazon had begun to apply AI robotic to replace some warehouse workers' tasks.

For another factory manufacture working environment example, AI can replace many manufacture workers to do their tasks in factories. Route 9 skims by Boston and cuts clear across Massachusetts to Pittsfield, a city of roughly 50,000, the largest in Berkshire County. Well east of Pittsfield, Route 9 becomes Worcester Road, named for a city that in earlier times was the nation's largest manufacturer of wire—barbed wire, electrical wire, telephone wire and the wire used in the making of undergarments by the Royal Worcester Corset Co., once the largest employer of women in the United States. Older Worcester residents can still recall the factory bells pealing to signal the start and end of the workday. Now, the bells are silent, and the wire and corset factories have been replaced with three of the nation's largest employers: Walmart, Target and Home Depot. If this sounds familiar, it should. It has been nearly two decades since retail overtook manufacturing as the nation's most important job creator, employing roughly one of every 10 American workers—more people than in health care and construction combined. That's a lot of jobs.

Of course, not all retail jobs qualify as what most of us consider good jobs. Today, the average hourly wage for a nonsupervisory retail worker is $11.24, and less than half of retail workers receive benefits of any kind. Still, as a nation, we've come to a sort of uneasy peace with this trend. We know that manufacturing employs far fewer Americans today than it once did—that iPads and Macs aren't made in America and neither are many televisions, appliances, tools, toys or clothes. We also know that shopping for these appliances, tools, toys and clothes is an all-American pastime: On average, we spend nearly 45 minutes a day (more than 270 hours per year) purchasing goods and services. Retail has become the world as we know it, and many of us expect to make our living working in that world.Thanks to automation and a killer business model, Amazon is so efficient that it reaps nearly twice the revenue per employee of Walmart, despite the fact that Walmart, too, has a substantial online presence. Worldwide, Amazon has installed over 100,000 robots to labor in "perfect symbiosis" with humans in its warehouses and has plans to install many thousands more. While it's not clear what constitutes perfect symbiosis, the robots are said to save the company $22 million annually, per warehouse. The company's master plan of an autonomous future also includes goods delivered by drones and self-driving vehicles.

For while Amazon continues to open warehouses around the globe and staff them with many thousands of human beings, estimates are that every human on the Amazon payroll—whether full- or part-time—displaces two humans at traditional brick-and-mortar operations. And that's a feature, not a bug: As Tim Lindner, a veteran IT analyst, confided in a note to industry insiders, eradicating jobs is the explicit goal of any online retailer. As he once wrote: "Labor is the highest-cost factor in warehouse operations. It is no secret that Amazon is moving to highly automated operations within its distribution centers, and...it has additional technology that can further reduce the number of humans it needs to process customer orders.... You have heard the old programmer's phrase, 'Garbage in, garbage out.'... [With] the diminishing reading abilities of humans on the Receiving dock, finding an automated solution to eliminate the 'garbage in' problem is the holy grail. Amazon may have just patented it."

By garbage, Lindner meant human error, the alternative to which is apparently robotic precision. And robots can be very precise, especially when it comes to routine tasks. Sawyer, an industrial robot created by the former Boston-based Rethink Robotics, offers an impressive illustration of how all-embracing a robot arm can be. Sawyer is the brainchild of Rodney Brooks, the inventor of both Roomba, the robotic vacuum, and PackBot, the robot used to clear bunkers in Iraq and Afghanistan and at the World Trade Center after 9/11. Unlike Roomba and PackBot, Sawyer looks almost human—it has an animated flat-screen face and wheels where its legs should be. Simply grabbing and adjusting its monkey-like arm and guiding it through a series of motions "teaches" Sawyer whatever repeatable procedure one needs it to get done. The robot can sense and manipulate objects almost as quickly and as fluidly as a human and demands very little in return: While traditional industrial robots require costly engineers and programmers to write and debug their code, a high school dropout can learn to program Sawyer in less than five minutes. Brooks once estimated that, all told, Sawyer (and his older brother, the two-armed Baxter robot) would work for a "wage" equivalent of less than $4 an hour.

Robots loom large in discussions of work and its future, a conversation that can get mired in false assumptions. Until recently, many economists were skeptical that automation could permanently displace human workers on a large scale. People have always shifted away from work better done by machines, but the economic principle of "comparative advantage" predicts that humans will maintain an edge in many fields. Under this logic, technology will not displace us but set us free to do less dangerous, more challenging things, essentially the very things that make humans human. Of course, human workers are complicated. We get tired, hungry, distracted, angry, confused. We make mistakes, sometimes egregious ones. Machines lack our frailties and biases and are better equipped to weigh evidence fairly, without prejudice or false assumptions. Perhaps most critically, machines can retain and process data far more accurately than we can, and that data is growing exponentially.

Every minute of every day, Google services 3.6 million searches in the United States alone. Spammers send 100 million emails. Snapchatters send 527,000 photos, and the Weather Channel broadcasts 18 million forecasts. This and more data—properly collected, codified and analyzed—can be applied to automate almost any high-order task. Data can also serve as a surrogate for human experience and intuition. Online shopping and social media sites "learn" our preferences and use that information to make values-based assessments to influence our decisions and behavior. And, increasingly, machines excel in the tasks once thought uniquely human."Computers are able to see and hear, and have face-recognition capabilities that are significantly better than humans," says Vardi. "Machines understand the human world far better than they did just a few years ago. And we haven't discovered anything in the human brain that can't be modeled."

● AI can replace counter cashier service staffs

And robots need not be perfect, only equal to—or a tad better than—complicated and expensive humans. And technologists are working hard to make sure they are a tad better. For example, in the case of retail, it's become clear that many of us avoid the self-service checkout line—we prefer the cashier to punch in our purchases rather than do so ourselves. So it seems that the job of cashier—among the largest retail employment categories—is not directly at risk. But Zeynep Ton, an MIT management expert who focuses on the retail sector, says self-service checkout is only a first step and not a terribly smart one. "Customers recognized that self-service checkout is not an innovation, but merely a way of outsourcing the job to them, so they didn't like it," she says. "But new technology is coming that will make self-service checkout so much easier and faster, and that will have a real impact on retail employment."

Experts caution that the so-called apocalypse in retail predicted a few years ago has not yet come to pass. In fact, for every company closing existing stores, two more are opening new stores. Retail is a highly competitive industry, and technology is transforming not only the way we shop but the way we connect with brands—for example, just a few years ago, who would have imagined that Amazon would open actual retail stores? And while e-commerce has grown to 10 percent of retail, that still leaves 90 percent for brick-and-mortar stores. But those brick-and-mortar stores, too, are undergoing radical change that has serious implications for America's workforce.

As example, Lobaugh cites food trucks, which he says increasingly pose a threat to many fast-food outlets. Unlike restaurants pinned down by a pair of Golden Arches, food trucks are nimble—they can home in on areas where customers are most likely to gather at any particular time. They can also tailor their offerings to a particular region or even a neighborhood, as well as use Facebook or other media to get out the word on their menu items and locations. Small, specialty stores also have far more flexibility than large department stores. "Technology has reduced the cost of entry into new markets, so in retail there are fewer big, monolithic companies, but more small competitors," he says. "Companies are diversifying to meet the specific needs and desires of consumers—everyone's piece is getting smaller, but there are many more pieces."

But despite what it predicts will be a banner holiday season, this year Amazon took on far fewer seasonal employees than usual—100,000 employees versus 120,000 the previous two years. And while an Amazon spokeswoman insisted that automation is not a factor in this reduced workforce, others seem to not agree. In a recent report, Morgan Stanley analyst Brian Nowak soothed the fears of Amazon shareholders concerned with the wage increase by pointing out that automation had already and would continue to reduce the call for labor, and therefore reduce overall costs. When asked about this, Lobaugh again tactfully declined to comment—other than to say that while the retail sector had lost less ground than most people assume, retail employees were another matter. "There are winners," he says, "and then there are losers."

● AI can replace accountants in accountancy service industry

Not that long ago artificial intelligence (AI), robots and machine learning (ML) were thought to be things only found in science fiction films. Today, this type of technology is taking center stage in workplaces across the globe. Industries, including manufacturing, retail, agriculture, and customer service have already had AI replace some job positions that left workers scrambling to find new career options. This AI revolution is not expected to slow down anytime soon. In fact, experts anticipate that as many as 800 million jobs could be replaced with AI technology by the year 2030. Initially, AI technology and automation in the workplace seemed to only affect pink and blue-collar workers. As this technology advances and becomes more powerful, professional, white-collar workers, including accountants, are starting to worry about what the future holds for their career and if AI will be developed to own their professional skills in accounting service industry.

In basic terms, AI technology is intelligent machines that are able to complete repetitive, mundane tasks at a fraction of the time it takes humans and with greater accuracy. The emergence of Machine Learning now allows AI platforms to observe, analyze and self-learn data and processes to improve its performance and accuracy over time. AI technology is already able to handle many accounting functions, such as tax preparation, payroll, and audits. Many of the leading accounting software providers, including Xero, Intuit and Sage have incorporated AI technology into their software to handle basic accounting tasks, such as bank reconciliations, invoice categorization, risk assessment, and audit processes, like expense submissions and invoice payments. Many of these standard tasks are extremely time-consuming, which has many accountants across the country worried about how the emerging AI technology will affect their billable hours. An even bigger concern is that AI technologies will replace the need for companies to work with accountants at all.

● AI Will Transform not Replace Accountants

While there is no doubt that AI technology is capable of handling many standard accounting tasks faster and more efficiently or that these capabilities will only increase over time, it doesn't mean the end for accountants. There always will be a need for that human element - human intelligence - at the other end of AI technology. In fact, according to leading research firm, Gartner, AI is set to create more jobs than it will replace, leaving workers, including accountants with options. Accountants don't have to worry about their job being replaced by AI any time in the near future. Companies will always need accountants that can analyze and interpret AI data, as well as provide consulting services. Rather than replacing the role of an accountant, AI technology will transform the duties an accountant performs.

With AI technology and machine learning handling many of the mundane, repetitive tasks, accountants will have more time to focus on other aspects of the job, such as consulting and data analysis. This is good news for many accountants. Rather than spending hours completing menial tasks, accountants of the future will be able to use and analyze AI data to provide their clients with sound business solutions.

In many ways, AI will help accountants improve their services. AI technology will improve data entry accuracy and lower the liability risk for accountants. In addition, emerging technology is more efficient at fraud detection, adding an extra layer of protection for accountants and their clients. It also provides real-time data, which allows accountants to provide real-time solutions. Even more impressive is the ability of machine learning to analyze large amounts of data instantly, evaluate past successes and failures in an effort to accurately predict future outcomes.

There is no way to escape the use of AI technology, at least not if you hope to remain competitive in the upcoming years. The speed, efficiency and accuracy of AI technology just cannot be beat. The only thing accountants can do is to embrace this new technology and learn how to maximize its use. The better equipped you are to help your clients integrate and utilize AI technology in their accounting processes the more valuable you will be. For example, many universities today are already incorporating IT and database management courses into their accounting program. This means that graduating students are coming into the workforce with the skills they need for future accounting work. Accountants already in the workforce must find ways to acquire these skills in order to remain relevant to their employers and/or their clients. Accountants can obtain the IT skills they need by attending seminars, using self-learning online programs or attending college-level courses. It is equally important for accountants to stay up-to-date on the latest accounting trends, emerging technologies and industry news. This will allows accountants to not only keep their jobs but to also provide more efficient services to their clients. Rather than worry about AI taking over their jobs, accountants should embrace this technology as a powerful solution to enhance customer services. Finally, accountants will be able to use all their training and experience to provide customer will real and effective business solutions, whether it's in reference to tax consulting, real estate deals, mergers, growth options, or any other business practice.

On conclusion, technology is advancing at record rates so now is the time to obtain the IT and database management skills you need to advance into the future. With the right skills and training, accountants are guaranteed a lucrative career that will last well into the future.

Why Developed And Developing Countries Need Artificial Intelligent Development To Assist Office Tasks

Must developed and developing countries need artificial intelligent development to assist office tasks ? Ought AI is needed to prefer to develop technique to assist office staffs to reduce workload to compare other kinds of occupation environment tasks aspects ? If one developed country, e.g. US, UK , Japan , Singapore it does not continue to develop artificial intelligence, robotic, then what disadvantges or weaknesses , it will encounter to compare when it chooses to continue to develop this artificial intelligent technology in society. If one developing country, e.g. China, Korea, Taiwan, it does not continue to develop artificial intelligence, robotic, then what disadantages or weaknesses, it will also encounter to compare when it chooses to continue to develop this artificial intelligent technology in in society. I shall explan the reasons why the results may cause to either the developed country, or the developing country as below:

● How AI help developing countries to communication and agriculture and learning and medical delivery development

Why can AI help developing countries ? Drones that pick inaccessible crops and mobile phones that give medical advice are two of the ways AI can transform life in the developing world. Artificial intelligence (AI) may improve the lives of the world's poor, the technology needed to revolutionise inefficient, ineffective food and healthcare systems in developing countries is well. For example, in low-income areas, agriculture and healthcare are two critical ecosystems that we can apply AI to immediately; this is not the far future, or even in five years.

Artificial intelligence (AI) has seeped into the daily lives of people in the developed world. From virtual assistants to recommendation engines, AI is in the news, our homes and offices. There is a lot of potential in terms of AI usage, especially in humanitarian areas. The impact could have a multiplier effect in developing countries, where resources are limited.

Emergency Response to developing countries' earthquake natural damage suddence occurrence predicting

AI and machine learning are still finding importance in emerging markets, but certain applications have emerged and are now widely used. For instance, predictive models for disaster relief enable first responders to automatically analyze large-scale behavior and movement through multiple sources of data including social media platforms, web forums, news sources, etc. Based on collected data, responders can scale reconstruction efforts and distribute supplies in a timely manner.

Why and how AI can assist farmers to predict when the earthquake occurs suddenly in order to avoid or reduce the natural damage to their agriculture productive number loss. For example, In 2015, when a major earthquake hit Nepal, more than 8 million people were affected. During the aftermath, drones were used to map and assess the destruction and speed up the rescue mission. The town of Sankhu, situated about 20 kilometers northeast of Kathmandu, was among the highly affected locations. In May 2018, my company Fusemachines and GeoSpatial Systems partnered with Sankhu's city officials to use drones and artificial intelligence in an effort to automatically estimate the reconstruction need. After processing data accumulated from a drone-powered aerial mapping of the region, the team fed this data to advanced machine learning algorithms. Combining drone imagery, digital mapping and machine learning, the team configured region modeling and infrastructure development with higher accuracy. Another organization known as One Concern, a California-based startup, has created a predictive AI program called Seismic Concern to accurately predict seism and is also working on solutions for wildfires, floods and hurricanes.

Smart AI Agriculture

Another application of AI in developing countries is smart agriculture. Farmers monitor crops more effectively and make better predictions on planting, weeding and harvesting using AI tools. It can also be used to analyze one plant at a time and add pesticides only to infected plants and trees instead of spraying pesticides across large swaths of crops. One California-based tech company is an example of this use of AI. So, the developing countries farmers in rural parts of India are also using AI to increase yields through better access to information about the farming season than they would normally have. Technology-enabled process automation offers the agribusiness industry the chance for remarkable growth -- not only in developed countries but around the world. There's a unique opportunity to increase yields, cut down labor costs and improve people's health.

Medicine Delivery to developing countries' patients urgent need

Companies are also leveraging AI to improve access to health care in some of the most remote areas of the world. In Rwanda, for example, Zipline is using drones to deliver medical supplies and blood to hospitals and clinics that are difficult to access by car. This has dramatically impacted people living in remote parts of the country because they are able to get medical help when needed. The drone system in Rwanda has also helped reduce waste of blood by 95%, as noted by Zipline. One Concern has created an AI program called Seismic Concern that accurately predicts seismic events and is also working on solutions for floods, wildfires and hurricanes. The medical field may actually benefit the most from emerging technologies in developing countries.

Assistance to reduce teaching work workload or psychological pressure to teachers in developing countries' schools

Another vital area benefiting from innovative technologies like AI is education. Advanced technologies can enhance how we learn, teach and perform tasks. In most developing countries, schools lack experienced teachers and resources to enhance students' knowledge. As a result, many students still have to walk long distances to get to the nearest school, which has created education gaps, especially in rural areas. AI tools such as personalized learning assistants can simplify learning by making tutoring services and learning materials accessible to all students, wherever they are. Machines can be automated to help students learn basic concepts without a tutor, which companies like Carnegie Learning are working on. This would allow students to learn at any time from anywhere. With AI, education is made easy and accessible to more people.

The initial usage of AI in developing countries has been at a micro level -- solving small, specific problems in a defined industry. As machine learning advances and there is a higher utilization of AI, we will see more complex issues being targeted and resolved. When duly adopted, AI can positively impact future developing countries people everyday lives not just in disaster intervention, education, health care and agriculture but can also help in mitigating poverty, malnutrition and pollution. Especially, in developing nations, to leverage AI's true potential and create a snowball effect. Startups are defining a holistic and humanitarian approach to building more sophisticated, AI-ready societies. Stakeholders in the AI landscape should understand the strengths and nuances of the developing world as well as the limitations of AI and create localized solutions and applications.

Why does smart phone help developing countries communication ? Internet Seen as Positive Influence on Education but Negative on Morality in Emerging and Developing Nations. Internet access differs substantially across the 32 emerging and developing countries polled, with the lowest rates of internet use in South Asian and sub-Saharan African nations. Within countries, computer owners, young people, the well-educated, the wealthy and those with English language ability are much more likely to access the internet than their counterparts. To access the internet, people increasingly use smartphones rather than more cumbersome fixed landline connections and computers. Around the world, both smartphones and basic-feature phones alike are used for sending messages and taking pictures.

In fact, many developing countries young people, students are popular to use smart phones for internet usage aim, instead of communication. Moreover, many developing countries working people are also popular to use smart phones for any working usage in their working time , even non working time any time. So, smart phones (AI) phones will be important communication or leisure tools to developing countries people in the future. Unless, it is one day, scientists can develop another new communication tool to replace smart phones. So, artificial intelligence will be important to influence developing countries people , how to improve or bring positive learning attitudes to students in their daily learnnng lifes. as well as how to raise developing countries people, how to raise working people efficiency or improve performace in their daily working lifes. So, AI may bring positive learning or working attitudes to developing countries working people and students both.

The Positive Impact of Mass Media in Developing Countries
Radio, newspapers, television, Internet, social media, etc., all of these are forms of mass media. Each of these outlets has the capability of bringing information to thousands of people with one device. While in some communities it is easy to take advantage of these communication outlets such as television and Internet access, not everyone has access to such outlets. Radio is one of the most common forms of mass media in developing countries because it's affordable and uses less electricity than many other forms of mass media, but only approximately 75 percent of people in developing countries have access to a radio, and roughly 77 percent of people in rural areas have access to electricity.

For developing countries that have implemented forms of mass media in their communities, there have been numerous positive outcomes are influenced to impact developing countries mass media by artificial intelligence as below:

When AI is participated to developing countries mass media, it can influence any radio, television audiences raise more attention to each other through social media platforms such as Facebook and Twitter and create, organize and initiate street protests and campaigns. Furthermore, having access to social media in developing countries, people are able to connect to those that they usually wouldn't have the chance to talk to. Moreover, AI Provides educational opportunities- In many countries, the division between local and national languages as well as issues of literacy can make communication difficult. With the use of mass media, a bridge can be built between these two gaps. In India, there is a radio station that provides information in local languages and respects local culture and traditions. One of the main ways is to create public awareness of what is going on with businesses and government officials. The media plays an important role in giving people the opportunity to act against injustice, oppression and misdeeds that they otherwise wouldn't know about. Information on available healthcare, a mass radio broadcast was sent out encouraging parents to seek treatment at local healthcare facilities for their sick children. With this mass outreach on healthcare, the encouragement of people to take their children to healthcare facilities saved thousands of lives. This easy way of encouraging others and bringing awareness about certain diseases was made possible through a simple radio broadcast. Finally, when AI is particiapted to media, it may bring many social issues to life that otherwise would remain unknown to many people. In developing countries and communities like Burkina Faso, when the radio broadcast was released about malaria, diarrhea and pneumonia, people were educated and moved to action and knew to take their children to healthcare facilities for preventative care. As it is seen, having access to different media outlets is vital for those in developing countries. Here are three ways that those in developing countries can implement mass media to help their people and communities.

When AI is participated to any internet radio or internet newspaper mass online listening or reading channel. It can provide online radios or newspapers in public places- By providing online radios and newspapers in public areas it gives community members to access news, information and emergency warnings. Even though radios can be on the cheaper side, there are still many people that can't afford to have a radio in their home. By providing one in a local place, not only would it better educate the community members but also it will bring the community together. So, it can make media outlets a two-way platform- Creating a two-way platform between the community and those who are behind the radio stations, newspapers or broadcasts makes the community feel involved and that their voices are being heard. An organization called Soul City in sub-Saharan Africa is showing how well two-way platforms work by engaging their listeners and having them contribute thoughts and ideas about complex issues. Because developing countries radio listening audiences or newspaper readers are popular to accept computer online radio listening channel or online newspaper reading channel to replace traditional paper newspapers or radio machines. So, AI may raise their listening news or reading news leisure feeling from online mass media channel in the future.

● Why do developed countries need to develop AI

Artificial intelligence, or AI, is driving massive shifts across the globe, and every day more questions arise. What impact will AI have on the workforce and how can we prepare for it? How can we encourage economy-boosting and job-creating technologies? How can we ensure that AI will be implemented ethically and with minimal bias? How will society benefit?

For developed country, such as US example. None of the US, Israel and Russia have a formal national AI policy yet. Private sector companies such as Google, Amazon and Apple and the US department of defence are driving the bulk of AI investment in the United States. Though Israel does not have a specific policy, it is keenly focused on AI and has seen the number of AI start-ups triple since 2014.

Developed country may learn whether what weakness it is lacking when it does not continue to develop AI from one another developed country. Which countries are approaching AI most effectively, and to what degree is there opportunity for greater international collaboration? It may be too early to tell; however, when analyzing the best practices of existing national AI policies, there is much that can be learned. These are the specific areas to consider. When one developed country continue to develop or research AI, it may bring these benefits as below:

On gathering Data aspect, from self-driving vehicles to smart cities, data is the driver behind AI. Innovation in the United States is limited without a national strategy that answers questions about protocol and ownership. France and Denmark, on the other hand, are opening government data. France is hosting troves of centrally collected public and private data that it plans to make available as part of its strategy. Conversely, by taking a restrictive position on issues of data collection (as indicated by the implementation of General Data Protection Regulation), the EU is putting manufacturers and software designers at a disadvantage while balancing the demand for privacy. On raising technologica talent aspect, the demand for AI talent far outweighs the available supply. As a result, almost every nation's strategy addresses talent development. Canada's AI strategy is distinct in that it primarily focuses on research and talent strategy. The country boasts AI degree programmes and is building a $127 million research facility in Toronto. Companies like Facebook and my own company, Uptake, are investing in Canada to access this talent pool. On AI legal technological innovation aspect, a whole host of legal questions swirl around AI. The country is developing a bill for AI liability that will be ready in March 2019. The government hopes the legal framework will attract investors by providing a simple, comprehensive guideline to enable the broad use of AI systems. So, when the developed country applied AI technology to assist any lawyers to work, then AI can help them to reduce the workload to draft any legal documents more easier. So, any developed countries lawyers' draft legal documents time must reduce if the developed countries lawyers accept to apply AI to assist their legal works. One of the great promises of AI is its potential for improving quality of life. But without the right planning and oversight, we risk exacerbating problems of inequality or marginalizing groups of people. As an example, India's AI strategy is focused on leveraging the technology not only for economic growth, but also for social inclusion.

AI may bring what benefits to developed countries

From SIRI to self-driving cars, artificial intelligence (AI) is progressing rapidly. While science fiction often portrays AI as robots with human-like characteristics, AI can encompass anything from Google's search algorithms to IBM's Watson to autonomous weapons. Artificial intelligence today is properly known as narrow AI (or weak AI), in that it is designed to perform a narrow task (e.g. only facial recognition or only internet searches or only driving a car). However, the long-term goal of many researchers is to create general AI (AGI or strong AI). While narrow AI may outperform humans at whatever its specific task is, like playing chess or solving equations, AGI would outperform humans at nearly every cognitive task.

Why research AI safety? Would AI bring war when AI is continued to develop by developed countries? In the near term, the goal of keeping AI's impact on society beneficial motivates research in many areas, from economics and law to technical topics such as verification, validity, security and control. Whereas it may be little more than a minor nuisance if your laptop crashes or gets hacked, it becomes all the more important that an AI system does what you want it to do if it controls your car, your airplane, your pacemaker, your automated trading system or your power grid. Another short-term challenge is preventing a devastating arms race in lethal autonomous weapons.

In the long term, an important question is what will happen if the quest for strong AI succeeds and an AI system becomes better than humans at all cognitive tasks. As pointed out by I.J. Good in 1965, designing smarter AI systems is itself a cognitive task. Such a system could potentially undergo recursive self-improvement, triggering an intelligence explosion leaving human intellect far behind. By inventing revolutionary new technologies, such a superintelligence might help us eradicate war, disease, and poverty, and so the creation of strong AI might be the biggest event in human history. Some experts have expressed concern, though, that it might also be the last, unless we learn to align the goals of the AI with ours before it becomes superintelligent.

There are some who question whether strong AI will ever be achieved, and others who insist that the creation of superintelligent AI is guaranteed to be beneficial. At FLI we recognize both of these possibilities, but also recognize the potential for an artificial intelligence system to intentionally or unintentionally cause great harm. We believe research today will help us better prepare for and prevent such potentially negative consequences in the future, thus enjoying the benefits of AI while avoiding pitfalls.

How can AI be dangerous when developed countries continue to develop AI to become weapon to replace soldiers?

Most researchers agree that a superintelligent AI is unlikely to exhibit human emotions like love or hate, and that there is no reason to expect AI to become intentionally benevolent or malevolent. Instead, when considering how AI might become a risk, experts think two scenarios most likely:

The AI is programmed to do something devastating: Autonomous weapons are artificial intelligence systems that are programmed to kill. In the hands of the wrong person, these weapons could easily cause mass casualties. Moreover, an AI arms race could inadvertently lead to an AI war that also results in mass casualties. To avoid being thwarted by the enemy, these weapons would be designed to be extremely difficult to simply "turn off," so humans could plausibly lose control of such a situation. This risk is one that's present even with narrow AI, but grows as levels of AI intelligence and autonomy increase.

The AI is programmed to do something beneficial, but it develops a destructive method for achieving its goal: This can happen whenever we fail to fully align the AI's goals with ours, which is strikingly difficult. If you ask an obedient intelligent car to take you to the airport as fast as possible, it might get you there chased by helicopters and covered in vomit, doing not what you wanted but literally what you asked for. If a superintelligent system is tasked with a ambitious geoengineering project, it might wreak havoc with our ecosystem as a side effect, and view human attempts to stop it as a threat to be met. So, a super-intelligent AI will be extremely good at accomplishing its goals, and if those goals aren't aligned with ours, we have a problem. You're probably not an evil ant-hater who steps on ants out of malice, but if you're in charge of a hydroelectric green energy project and there's an anthill in the region to be flooded, too bad for the ants. A key goal of AI safety research is to never place humanity in the position of those ants.

Why the recent interest in AI safety ?

Stephen Hawking, Elon Musk, Steve Wozniak, Bill Gates, and many other big names in science and technology have recently expressed concern in the media and via open letters about the risks posed by AI, joined by many leading AI researchers. The idea that the quest for strong AI would ultimately succeed was long thought of as science fiction, centuries or more away. However, thanks to recent breakthroughs, many AI milestones, which experts viewed as decades away merely five years ago, have now been reached, making many experts take seriously the possibility of superintelligence in our lifetime. While some experts still guess that human-level AI is centuries away, most AI researches at the 2015 Puerto Rico Conference guessed that it would happen before 2060. Since it may take decades to complete the required safety research, it is prudent to start it now.

Because AI has the potential to become more intelligent than any human, we have no surprise way of predicting how it will behave. We can't use past technological developments as much of a basis because we've never created anything that has the ability to, wittingly or unwittingly, outsmart us. The best example of what we could face may be our own evolution. People now control the planet, not because we're the strongest, fastest or biggest, but because we're the smartest. If we're no longer the smartest, are we assured to remain in control?

A captivating conversation is taking place about the future of artificial intelligence and what it will/should mean for humanity. There are fascinating controversies where the world's leading experts disagree, such as: AI's future impact on the job market; if/when human-level AI will be developed; whether this will lead to an intelligence explosion; and whether this is something we should welcome or fear. But there are also many examples of of boring pseudo-controversies caused by people misunderstanding and talking past each other. When one developed country continue to develop AI, can itself country's all factories workers will lose jobs, due to AI can replace them to do simple works in factories, or any public transport drivers, e.g. bus drivers, ferry , tram, train drivers, they will lose jobs, when AI (non manual driving drivers) can replace all public transport drivers. So, some occupations will lose if developed countries continue to develop or research AI to replace human to do some simple jobs, such as some cooking jobs can be done by AI. So, it is possible that future cookers won't be needed, because AI cooking skills may be better than them to cook any good taste chinese or western food in restaurants.

If you drive down the road, you have a subjective experience of colors, sounds, etc. But does a self-driving car have a subjective experience? Does it feel like anything at all to be a self-driving car? Although this mystery of consciousness is interesting in its own right, it's irrelevant to AI risk. If you get struck by a driverless car, it makes no difference to you whether it subjectively feels conscious. In the same way, what will affect us humans is what superintelligent AI does, not how it subjectively feels.

In fact, AI may be make any brokers jobs in financial market. the main concern of the beneficial-AI movement isn't with robots but with intelligence itself: specifically, intelligence whose goals are misaligned with ours. To cause us trouble, such misaligned superhuman intelligence needs no robotic body, merely an internet connection – this may enable outsmarting financial markets, out-inventing human researchers, out-manipulating human leaders, and developing weapons we cannot even understand. Even if building robots were physically impossible, a super-intelligent and super-wealthy AI could easily pay or manipulate many humans to unwittingly do its bidding. So, future brokers will be replaced by AI, when AI can be made to own financial brokers' analytical mind to make more accurate whether the share price will rise up or fall down to compare human financial brokers' analytical mind. The robot misconception is related to the myth that machines can't control humans. Intelligence enables control: humans control tigers not because we are stronger, but because we are smarter. This means that if we cede our position as smartest on our planet, it's possible that we might also cede control.

Not wasting time on the above-mentioned misconceptions lets us focus on true and interesting controversies where even the experts disagree. What sort of future do you want? Should we develop lethal autonomous weapons? What would you like to happen with job automation? What career advice would you give today's kids? Do you prefer new jobs replacing the old ones, or a jobless society where everyone enjoys a life of leisure and machine-produced wealth? Further down the road, would you like us to create superintelligent life and spread it through our cosmos? Will we control intelligent machines or will they control us? Will intelligent machines replace us, coexist with us, or merge with us? What will it mean to be human in the age of artificial intelligence?

Why do developed countries people need AI ?

Why do we assume that AI will require more and more physical space and more power when human intelligence continuously manages to miniaturize and reduce power consumption of its devices. How low the power needs and how small will the machines be by the time quantum computing becomes reality? Why do we assume that AI will exist as independent machines? If so, and the AI is able to improve its Intelligence by reprogramming itself, will machines driven by slower processors feel threatened, not by mere stupid humans, but by machines with faster processors? What would drive machines to reproduce themselves when there is no biological incentive, pressure or need to do so?

Who says superior AI will need or want to have a physical existence when an immaterial AI could evolve and preserve itself better from external dangers. What will happen if AI developed by competing ideologies, liberalism vs communism, reach maturity at the same time, will they fight for hegemony by trying to destroy each other physically and/or virtually. If AI is programmed to believe in God, and competing AI emerges programmed by muslims, christians or jews, how are the different AI's going to make sense of the different religious beliefs, are we going to have AI religious wars? What if the "powers that be" greatest fear is the emergence of a super AI that police's and rationalizes the distribution of wealth and food. A friendly super AI that is programmed to help humanity by, enforcing the declaration of Human Rights (the US is the only industrialized country that to this day has not signed this declaration) ending corruption and racism and protecting the environment.Most benefits of civilization stem from intelligence, so how can we enhance these benefits with artificial intelligence without being replaced on the job market and perhaps altogether?

Key to the process of machine learning are neural networks. These are brain-inspired networks of interconnected layers of algorithms, called neurons, that feed data into each other, and which can be trained to carry out specific tasks by modifying the importance attributed to input data as it passes between the layers. During training of these neural networks, the weights attached to different inputs will continue to be varied until the output from the neural network is very close to what is desired, at which point the network will have 'learned' how to carry out a particular task. A subset of machine learning is deep learning, where neural networks are expanded into sprawling networks with a huge number of layers that are trained using massive amounts of data. It is these deep neural networks that have fuelled the current leap forward in the ability of computers to carry out task like speech recognition and computer vision.

In conclusion, when developed countries continue to develop AI, it may bring positive advantages to bring raising productivies, or efficiencies, but it may also raise unemployment ratio to any low skill or low knowledge jobs in ther societies. However, human future society will need to change to be better to raise our living standard. But AI is one kind the best choice tool to achieve this aim in our future, so I agree developed countries continue to develop or research AI to be the super -human machine.

Artificial Intelligence Worker Brings

Working Environment Influences

Robots were once known only for the manufacturing business but today they are very much part of many workplaces. The future is even more promising for this wonder of artificial intelligence.Imagine a robot doing some of the major tasks of managers like using data to evaluate problems, making better decisions, monitoring team performance, and even setting goals.

Technology is playing a pivotal role in helping humans work more effectively. Since automation has become an integral part of business operations, we can predict that robots are soon going to replace many jobs that are today performed by humans. Now that the corporate world is also on the cusp of entering the robotic age, let's see what pros and cons this technology offers business world. If one day, our global working environments have any kinds of robotic participates to our service and warehouse and office etc. different working environment in order to assist office workers, service workers, warehouse workers, professional lawyers, doctors accountants job duties, what positive or negative influences, it will bring to what negative or positive effects to any office , warehouse, shopping center, hospital, transport , restaurant etc, different working environments. Can robotic help office , warehouse to raise efficiency ? Can robotic help hospital, restaurant, cinema, shopping center to improve service performance? Can robotic influence working environment to be worse? Can robotic help office or any working places to reduce expenditure or reduce long time machine and salary cost when they do not need more employees or machines , due to robotic workers assistance.

I shall attempt to explain whether robotic workers will bring what positive or negative influence to our future working environment as below:

Advantages to robotic bring to working environment

What advantages that robotic will bring to working environment? They may include: Many people fear that robots or full automation may someday take their jobs, but this is simply not the case. Robots bring more advantages than disadvantages to the workplace. They enrich a company's ability to succeed while improving the lives of real, human employees who are still needed to keep operations running smoothly. If you're thinking about investing in some robots, share the advantages with your employees. You might be surprised at how many of them are quick to support the idea.

1. Safety

Safety is the most obvious advantage of utilizing robotics. Heavy machinery, machinery that runs at hot temperature, and sharp objects can easily injure a human being. By delegating dangerous tasks to a robot, you're more likely to look at a repair bill than a serious medical bill or a lawsuit. Employees who work dangerous jobs will be thankful that robots can remove some of the risks.

2. Speed

Robots don't get distracted or need to take breaks. They don't request vacation time or ask to leave an hour early. A robot will never feel stressed out and start running slower. They also don't need to be invited to employee meetings or training session. Robots can work all the time, and this speeds up production. They keep your employees from having to overwork themselves to meet high pressure deadlines or seemingly impossible standards.

3. Consistency

Robots never need to divide their attention between a multitude of things. Their work is never contingent on the work of other people. They won't have unexpected emergencies, and they won't need to be relocated to complete a different time sensitive task. They're always there, and they're doing what they're supposed to do. Automation is typically far more reliable than human labor.

4. Perfection

Robots will always deliver quality. Since they're programmed for precise, repetitive motion, they're less likely to make mistakes. In some ways, robots are simultaneously an employee and a quality control system. A lack of quirks and preferences, combined with the eliminated possibility of human error, will create a predictably perfect product every time.

5. Happier Employees

Since robots are often assigned to perform tasks that people don't particularly enjoy, like menial work, repetitive motion, or dangerous jobs, your employees are more likely to be happy. They'll be focusing on more engaging work that's less likely to grind down their nerves. They might want to take advantage of additional educational opportunities, utilize your employee wellness program, or participate in an innovative workplace project. They'll be happy to let the robots do the work that leaves them feeling burned out.

6. Job Creation

Robots don't take jobs away. They merely change the jobs that exist. Robots need people for monitoring and supervision. The more robots we need, the more people we'll need to build those robots. By training your employees to work with robots, you're giving them a reason to stay motivated in their position with your company. They'll be there for the advancements and they'll have the unique opportunity to develop a new set of tech or engineering related skills.

7. Productivity

Robots can't do everything. Some jobs absolutely need to be completed by a human. If your human employees aren't caught up doing the things that could have easily be left for robots, they'll be available and productive. They can talk to customers, answer emails and social media comments, help with branding and marketing, and sell products. You'll be amazed at how much they can accomplish when the grunt work isn't weighing them down.

8. Cost reduce

The first and the foremost advantage of having robots in workplaces is their cost. Robots are much cheaper than humans and their cost is now decreasing. It's a fact that we cannot compare human abilities with robots but robotic capabilities are now growing quickly. For example, if you run an essay writing service, you can use robots to perform every kind of research related to any subject. Because robots are more active and don't get tired like humans, the collaboration between humans and robots is reducing absenteeism. The pace of human cannot increase hence robots are helping humans.

However,robots are more precise than humans; they don't tremble or shake as human hands. Robots have smaller and versatile moving parts which help them in performing tasks with more accuracy than humans. There is no doubt that robots are significantly stronger and faster than humans. Robots come in any shape and size, depending upon the need of the task. Robots can work anywhere in any environmental condition whether it is space, underwater, in extreme heat or wind etc. Robots can be used everywhere where human safety is a huge concern. Robots are programmed by a human;

they cannot say no to anything and can be used for any dangerous and unwanted work where humans may deny to offer their services. For example, many robotic probes have been sent into space but have never returned. Robots in warfare are saving more lives and have now proven to be very successful. For example, in chemical factory environment, robots are now being used in the chemical industry and can, for example deal with chemical spills in a nuclear plant, which would otherwise pose a major health concern. Cost-effectiveness is one of the most sound arguments to be made for the case of industrial robots. Robots will reduce production costs by eliminating internal costs to compensate human salaries. Businesses are forecasting that their profitability will increase once they implement robots into production, or that they will have more financial mobility to invest in new products or technologies.

9. productive efficiency

Quality assurance is expected with the use of machinery in production. Industrial robots will be able to ensure consistency with mass production of manufactured products. The possible human error that assembly line workers pose the threat of will be removed. Optimized production efficiency means that a general manager will be able to have set quantity and quality standards that will be met by robots. Production quotas will not be jeopardized by low concentration, break time and employee injuries, among other things. The efficiency of production forecasts and supply levels will be increased with robots, able to be programmed to work at the optimal speed for a given plant. Limiting human work in hazardous environments, because manufacturing jobs often place workers at more physical risk compared to a lot of other industries. Lowering the level of a hazard presented to employees on the job is attractive to executives to preserve company reputation and minimize potential legal liabilities.

10. Reducing longer working hours

Typically people have to have breaks, get distracted and after time attention drops and pace slows. With a robot it can work 24/7, and keeps running at 100%. Typically if you replace one person on a key process in a production line with a robot the output increases by 40% in the same working hours just because a robot has more stamina and never stops. Robots also don't take holidays or have unexpected days off sick.

11. Increased profitability

By increasing the efficiency of your production process, reducing the resource and time needed to complete it, and also achieving higher quality products, industrial robots can thus be used to achieve higher profitability levels overall, with lower cost per product.

12. Improved working environment

Industrial robots are often used for performing tasks which are deemed as dangerous for humans, as well as being able to perform highly laborious and repetitive tasks. Overall, by using industrial robots you can improve the working conditions and safety in your factory or production process. Robots don't get tired and make dangerous mistakes, neither do they suffer from repetitive strain injury.Due to their high accuracy levels, robots can also be used to produce higher quality products which adhere to certain standards of quality, whilst also reducing the time needed for quality control.Industrial robots are able to complete certain tasks faster and better than people, as they are designed to perform these tasks with a higher accuracy level. This and the fact that they are used to automate processes which previously might have taken significantly more time and resources, means that you can often use industrial robots to increase the efficiency of your production line.

13. Improved Quality Assurance

Few workers enjoy doing repetitive tasks and after a certain period of time concentration levels will naturally decline. This lapse in concentration is known as vigilance decrement and can often lead to costly errors for the business and sometimes serious injury to the member of staff.Robotic automation eliminates these risks by accurately producing and checking items meet the required standard without fail. With more product going out the door manufactured to a higher standard, this creates a number of new business possibilities for companies to expand upon.

14. Increased Productivity

Using robotic automation to tackle repetitive tasks makes complete sense. Robots are designed to make repetitive movements. Humans, also by design, are not. The introduction of automation into your manufacturing process has many different productivity benefits, some of which are shown here.Giving staff members the opportunity to expand on their skills and work in other areas will create a better environment which the business as a whole will benefit from. With higher energy levels and more focus put into their work, the product can only improve, which will also lead to extremely satisfied clients.

15. Avoiding workers need to work In Hazardous Environments

Aside from potential injuries in the workplace, staff members in particular industries can be asked to work in unstable or dangerous environments. For example, if a high level of chemicals are present, robotic automation offers the ideal solution, as it will continue to work without harm. Production areas that require extremely high or low temperatures typically have a high turnover of staff due to the nature of the work. Automated robots can minimise material waste and remove the need for humans to put themselves at unnecessary risk.

Disadvantages to robotic bring to working environment

1. Increase unemployment rate and job loss

On working environment cost increasing aspect, where robots are increasing the efficiency in many businesses, they are also increasing the unemployment rate. Because of robots, human labour is no longer required in many factories and manufacturing plants. They can certainly handle their prescribed tasks, but they typically cannot handle unexpected situations.The ROI of your business may suffer if your operation relies on too many robots. They have higher expenses than humans, so at the end of the day you may not always achieve the desired ROI.

However, robots may have AI but they are certainly not as intelligent as humans. They can never improve their jobs outside the pre-defined programming because they simply cannot think for themselves. Robots installed in workplaces still require manual labour attached to them. Training those employees on how to work with the robots definitely has a cost attached to it.Moreover, robots have no sense of emotions or conscience. They lack empathy and this is one major disadvantage of having an emotionless workplace.Also, robots operate on the basis of information fed to them through a chip. If one thing goes wrong the entire company bears the loss. Where a robot saves times, on the other hand it can also result in a lag. It is, after all, a machine so you cannot expect too much from them. If a robot malfunctions, you need extra time to fix it, which would require reprogramming.If ultimately robots would do all the work, and the humans will just sit and monitor them, health hazards will increase rapidly. Obesity will be on top of the list. So there are advantages, but there are disadvantages as well. It is the twenty first century and we cannot work without machines.Humans are still considered far more efficient than robots when it comes to decision making powers, handling difficult situations, brainstorming, and generally bringing a sense of emotion and empathy into a workplace. Besides, you cannot rule out the significant role of humans in a business. After all, no machine can replace the human factor 'real employees' bring into a workplace. So, AI can raise unemployment and increase factory or shopping center or office working environment cost when their working environment are applied robotic to replace many workers, then machine electricity expense will also increase. Otherwise, human workers can not spend too much electricity expense in cost aspect.

Whilst industrial robots can prove highly effective and bring you a positive ROI, implementing them might require a fairly high capital cost. That's why, before making a decision we recommend considering both the investment needed and also the ROI you expect to achieve. Often the easiest way to get round this issue is to take out asset finance and the ROI of the robot more than pays for the interest on the asset finance.

This is typically the biggest obstacle that will decide whether or not a company will invest in robotic automation, or wait until a later stage. A comprehensive business case must be built when considering the implementation of this technology. The returns can be substantial and quite often occur within a short space of time. However, the cash flow must be sustainable in the meantime and the stability of the company is by no means worth the risk if the returns are only marginal. Yet, in most instances there will be a repayment schedule available, which makes it a lot easier to afford and control finances. Our downloadable automation payback calculator also has a finance scheme option so you can see how this would work for you.

On job loss increasing aspect, Job loss is by far the most significant opposition frequently brought against the use of robots in the manufacturing industry. Industry workers of all levels, from entry-level to veterans, worry about the security of their employment status, and the ability of their job to be replaced by a robot. This panic is more widespread in this industry compared to others because of the closer immanence of a robot takeover in manufacturing.

Macro effects are another topic that usually comes up with job loss. More "big picture" thinkers wonder how the national, and eventually global economy will be affected when manufacturing workers' jobs are displaced. How can this mass unemployment possibly be compensated for, and how can the robots' presumed success be limited from seeping into other industries. However, increased investment costs are a financial counterpoint to industrial robots, with the idea that manufacturing companies will rack up their debt investing in robotic technology. Firms that do not have the funding might even go bankrupt in an effort to keep up with industry trends rather than continue on with normalized operations.Hence, elimination of a whole labor class would presumably occur a bit of a ways down the road, but the implications of this point are too large not to consider. Bringing in robots to take unskilled labor jobs will place more pressure on the economy, education system, and financial market, just to name a few. The United States has always been associated with the grit and work ethic of its blue-collar workers, and robots are threatening to eliminate this aspect of the human population, with a take over of production jobs.

One of the biggest concerns surrounding the introduction of robotic automation is the impact of jobs for workers. If a robot can perform at a faster, more consistent rate, then the fear is that humans may not be needed at all. While these worries are understandable, they are not really accurate.The same was said during the early years of the industrial revolution, and as history has showed us, humans continued to play an essential role. Amazon are a great example of this. The employment rate has grown rapidly during a period where they have gone from using around 1,000 robots to over 45,000

2. Robotic can not perform better to compare human workers, when they need to work long time in any working environment

Robots need a supply of power, The people can lose jobs in factories, They need maintenance to keep them running, It costs a lot of money to make or buy robots, The software and the equipment that you need to use with the robot cost much money. Robots cost much money in maintenance & repair, The programs need to be updated to suit the changing requirements, the machines need to be made smarter, In case of breakdown, the cost of repair may be very high, The procedures to restore lost code or data may be time-consuming & costly.

Robots can store large amounts of data but the storage, access, retrieval is not as effective as the human brain, They can perform repetitive tasks for a long time but they do not get better with experience such as the humans do. Robots are not able to act any different from what they are programmed to do, With the heavy application of robots, the humans may become overly dependent on the machines, losing their mental capacities, If the control of robots goes in the wrong hands, Robots may cause the destruction. Robots are not intelligent or sentient, They can never improve the results of their jobs outside of their predefined programming, They do not think, They do not have emotions or conscience, This limits how the robots can help & interact with people. Robots can take the place of many humans in factories, So, the people have to find new jobs or be retrained, They can take the place of the humans in several situations, If the robots begin to replace the humans in every field, They will lead to unemployment.

Humans fear robots, Robots inspire two types of fear: firstly, that they might take over our jobs, and secondly, that they could take over the world, Robots will steal our jobs, Robots have the effect of increasing productivity rather than eliminating jobs.Robotics become increasingly present in our everyday life, with household robots, medical, industrial, on production lines, not to mention airports, banks, and hotels, So, Robots may dominate the human species. Robots can operate on the basis of information fed to them through a chip, when one thing goes wrong the entire company bears a loss.The robot can save times, but it can also result in a lag, It is a machine so you can't expect too much from them, If the robot has malfunctioned, you need extra time to fix it, which would require reprogramming, If robots would do all the work, and the humans will just sit and monitor them, health hazards will increase rapidly, Obesity will be on top of the list and less labour at workplaces.

3. Increasing training expense

Whilst industrial robots are excellent for performing many tasks, as with any other type of technology, they require more training and expertise to initially set up. The expertise of a good automation company with a support package will be very important. To minimise your reliance on automation companies you can train some of your engineers on how to program robots, but you will still need the assistance of experienced automation companies for the original integration of the robot.

In recent years the number of industrial robots and the applications they can be used for has increased significantly. However, there still are some limitations in terms of the type of tasks they can perform, which is why we suggest that an automation company looks at your requirement to assess the options first. Sometimes a bespoke automated system may give a better or faster result than a robot. Also, a robot does not have everything built into it, often the success or failure of an industrial robotic system depends on how well the surrounding systems are integrated e.g. grippers, vision systems, conveyor systems etc. Only use good trusted robot integrators to be sure of the optimum results if you do choose to use industrial robots.

Artificial intelligent working participation how brings economic growth

● How AI impacts economy

What is AI non-manual shops? Why and how it can assist economic growth? I shall explain as below:

Artificial Intelligence, as we see it, is a collection of multiple technologies that enable machines to sense, comprehend and act—and learn, either on their own or to augment human activities. Compelling data reveal a discouraging truth about growth today. There has been a marked decline in the ability of traditional levers of production—capital investment and labor—to propel economic growth. Artificial intelligence (AI) is a new factor of production and has the potential to introduce new sources of growth, changing how work is done and reinforcing the role of people to drive growth in business. Accenture research on the impact of AI in 12 developed economies reveals that AI could double annual economic growth rates in 2035 by changing the nature of work and creating a new relationship between man and machine. The impact of AI technologies on business is projected to increase labor productivity by up to 40 percent and enable people to make more efficient use of their time.

To fulfill the promise of AI as a new factor of production that can reignite growth, Accenture recommends the following steps be taken to help navigate the complexity of issues:

· Prepare the next generation – integrate human intelligence with machine intelligence so they can successfully co-exist in a two-way learning relationship and reevaluate the type of knowledge and skills required for the future.

· Encourage AI-powered regulation – update and create adaptive, self-improving laws to close the gap between the pace of technological change and the pace of regulatory response.

· Advocate a code of ethics for AI – ethical debates should be supplemented by tangible standards and best practices in the development and use of intelligent machines.

· Address the redistribution effects – policymakers should highlight how AI can result in tangible benefits and preemptively address any perceived downsides of AI, helping groups disproportionately affected by changes of employment and incomes.

Our research strongly shows that AI can unleash remarkable benefits across countries, countering slow economic growth and lagging productivity. To fulfill the promise of AI, relevant stakeholders must be thoroughly prepared – intellectually, technologically, politically, ethically and socially - to address the benefits and challenges that can arise as artificial intelligence becomes more integrated in our daily lives."

How AI impacts economy? AI has the potential to markedly increase industry growth. Information and Communication, Manufacturing and Financial Services are the three sectors that will benefit most from the application of AI. AI offers unprecedented profitability opportunities. For example, manufacturing has a forecast share-of-profit increase of 39 percent due to AI-powered systems whose ability to learn, adapt and evolve over time can eliminate faulty machines and idle equipment.

www.ingramcontent.com/pod-product-compliance
Lightning Source LLC
Chambersburg PA
CBHW060922140726
47996CB00001B/343